Logistics in Support of Disaster Relief

by

LTC James H. Henderson "Cotton", USA (Ret.)

authorHOUSE®

AuthorHouse™
1663 Liberty Drive, Suite 200
Bloomington, IN 47403
www.authorhouse.com
Phone: 1-800-839-8640

© 2007 LTC James H. Henderson "Cotton", USA (Ret.). All rights reserved.
No part of this book may be reproduced, stored in a retrieval system, or
transmitted by any means without the written permission of the author.

First published by AuthorHouse 10/18/2007

ISBN: 978-1-4343-3471-8 (e)
ISBN: 978-1-4343-3470-1 (sc)
ISBN: 978-1-4343-3469-5 (hc)

Library of Congress Control Number: 2007906791

Printed in the United States of America
Bloomington, Indiana

This book is printed on acid-free paper.

Sandy, I love you very much...Thanks!

Also, special thanks to Nash Nunnery, Jessica Smith and Walter Langley...they know why.

Contents

Preface		xiii
1.	Katrina	1
2.	Framework and Structure	7
3.	The Plan	13
4.	Operational Control	39
5.	Disaster Relief Support Management	51
6.	Building the Relief Support Network	59
7.	Relief Support Process	79
8.	Pre-Disaster Operations	85
9.	Initial Disaster Operations	93
10.	Sustainment of Disaster Operations	101
11.	Closure of Disaster Operations	107
12.	Thinking Out of the Box	115
Summary		119
Bibliography		121
Glossary		131

FIGURES

Figure 1, United States Interstate System — 9

Figure 2, United States Interstate Corridors, North to South and East to West — 11

Figure 3, Bands of Support — 28

Figure 4, Organizational Outlook for Successful Information Management — 40

Figure 5, Organizational Information Flow — 42

Figure 6, Information Flow Elements — 46

Figure 7, Example of building and/or tents — 48

Figure 8, Example 1, of a Mobile Operations Center Design — 49

Figure 9, Example 2, of a Mobile Operations Center Design — 50

Figure 10, Distribution Network Enablers — 60

Figure 11, Example of Road Network — 61

Figure 12, How Radio Frequency Identification (RFID) System Work — 63

Figure 13, Example of container marked with an Identification Bar Code Label and RIFD tag — 64

Figure 14, How Interrogator System Works — 65

Figure 15, Example of Fixed and Hand-held Interrogators — 66

Figure 16, Example of Placing Fixed and Hand-held Interrogators — 67

Figure 17, How Satellite Devices for Movement Tracking System Works   68

Figure 18, Example of Movement Tracking of multiple Transponders   69

Figure 19, Examples of Satellite Tracking Devices   70

Figure 20, Employment of Network Enablers for Movement Tracking   73

Figure 21, Network Enablers for Route and Distribution Management   74

Figure 22, Example of a Disaster Relief Support Physical Structure Lay Out   77

Figure 23, Linear Supply Routes from the Call Forward Area to the Forward Distribution Points   82

Figure 24, Nonlinear Supply Routes from the Call Forward Area to the different Forward Distribution Points and back.   83

Figure 25, Stage I: Pre-Disaster Operations (N-72 – N-48 hours)   86

Stage I– Planning Diagram Insert, Figure 26   87

Stage I– Synchronization Diagram Insert, Figure 27   88

Stage I– Implementation Diagram Insert, Figure 28   89

Stage I – In-Transit Visibility Diagram Insert, Figure 29   91

Figure 30, Stage II: Initial Disaster Operations (N-24 – N+96 hours)   94

Stage II – Planning Diagram Insert, Figure 31   95

Stage II – Synchronization Diagram Insert, Figure 32   96

Stage II – Implementation Diagram Insert Figure 33   97

Stage II– In-Transit Visibility Diagram Insert, Figure 34   99

Figure 35, Stage III: Sustainment of Disaster Operations   102

Stage III– Synchronization and Implementation Diagram Insert, Figure 36   103

Stage III– In-Transit Visibility Diagram Insert, Figure 37   105

Stage III– Planning Diagram Insert, Figure 38   106

Figure 39, Stage IV: Closure of Disaster Operations   108

Stage IV – Planning and Synchronization 1 Diagram Insert, Figure 40   109

Stage IV – In-Transit Visibility Diagram Insert Figure 41   111

Stage IV – Implementation Diagram Insert, Figure 42   112

Stage IV – Planning and Synchronization 2 Diagram Insert, Figure 43   114

PREFACE

In the days before Hurricane Katrina, I was at Fort Lee, Virginia, to conduct a Military Distribution Management Exercise for the U.S. Army Quartermaster and Transportation schools. My wife and family were at our home, an hour and half north of the Mississippi Gulf Coast in a small community named Baxterville, southwest of Hattiesburg, Mississippi. My wife, my youngest son, and our dog fared the brunt of the storm as it moved north through Mississippi. Our property looked like a war zone, trees were on the house and down all over the grounds, and there were sections of roof gone on other buildings located on the property. Following Hurricane Katrina, the Army requested assistance from Team Battle Command Sustainment Support System (BCS3) to support the 13th Sustainment Command (Expeditionary), from Fort Hood, Texas, and I traveled to Baton Rouge and ultimately New Orleans, Louisiana, to assist the logistical relief operations. Therefore, after only a week and half after returning home I was on the way to Louisianan for the next two weeks. I returned home only few days before landfall of Hurricane Rita and luckily, there was not another operation for the rest of the hurricane season.

It was in these circumstances, my wife, as she always has, did an amazing job in persevering, and I would like to dedicate this book to her and the actions she took to lead our family through both the hurricane and its aftermath.

Cotton

CHAPTER 1

Katrina

Perspective

To establish the foundation of "*Why*" this book came about and establish the relationship of the ideas and concepts in support of disaster support operations I must first state the events and circumstance that show my involvement to this subject. Again, this is not written to provide an overall answer to every situation, but instead to provide a basis to plan and coordinate at the federal, state, and local government levels as they develop and implement support operations.

On August 29, 2005, Hurricane Katrina overwhelmed the Mississippi and Louisiana gulf coast, and issues concerning emergency evacuation and disaster relief support became a huge requirement. One hundred and twenty mile an hour winds and rising water caused devastating damage. This book is not an account of the relief operations conducted in these areas, but a start for the ideas and concepts to support future planning, coordination, and development of *Logistical Disaster Relief Support Operation's* in the future.

Scenario

In the days leading up to Hurricane Katrina, my travels took me to Fort Lee, Virginia, to conduct a Military Distribution Management Exercise for the U.S. Army Quartermaster and Transportation schools. My wife and family were at our home, an hour and half north of the Mississippi Gulf Coast in a small community named Baxterville, southwest of Hattiesburg, Mississippi. That morning, I was conducting an exercise opening a Distribution Management class and had asked one of the Captain's in the front row to monitor the hurricane on the computer located at his desk, and to keep me updated on the hurricane tracking. My wife called at 0600 hours and advised me that the electricity and water had gone off, but that the phone was working. The phone company must have had a local emergency power, because the phones worked for about the next twelve hours. We spoke at 1600 hours and it was the last time we talked until four days after the hurricane had past our region. At that time my wife had moved the family two hours north, to my hometown of Clinton, Mississippi, where she had communications and most importantly electricity. Finally on that the fourth day, we talked and I advised her I would arrive at the Jackson Airport the next day. Upon leaving the airport there was a long line of vehicles on the shoulder of the road to my right. My wife informed me it was a gas line and we were getting close to empty so I quickly got in line. Three hours later, it was our turn to get gas; "it was crazy". One positive thing happened for my family just before we returned to our home, was that the water was reestablished. It was not potable, but we could use that water to bathe. We loaded up with provisions and two days later, we returned home, and met my wife's brother, who had traveled from Tallahassee, Florida, with a generator, forty gallons of gasoline and other assorted items to assist us in our personal recovery. Weeks later, after many hours with a chainsaw, as well as working on the roofs of the houses and barns, electricity was finally reestablished and we once again had air conditioning. That very afternoon my Blackberry rang, and it was the Program Manager of the Battle Command Sustainment Support System (BCS3), who informed me that three individuals were to arrive in Birmingham, Alabama, and would drive to my location and pick me up the next morning. We were to travel to Baton Rouge and ultimately New Orleans, Louisiana, to meet the 13th Sustainment Command (Expeditionary) (SC (E)), from Fort Hood, Texas to support them in logistical relief support operations mainly in the area of In-Transit Visibility (ITV).

Logistics in Support of Disaster Relief

Henderson's Role in Hurricane Katrina

It was around five o'clock in the afternoon when we arrived in Baton Rouge, LA, and it was hard to tell if the traffic was bad because of the dislocated victims of Hurricane Katrina or just their normal rush hour. The traffic is always bad going east or west through the city during rush hours, but I believe that Hurricane Katrina had a huge effect in that you could not tell a break in the traffic between morning and evening rush hours. There was consistent traffic all day for the two weeks when I was working in and around the area. One of the members from our team told us that coordination with the local U. S. Army Reserve Center had been made, it was on the north side of the city as if you were going to the airport, and that we could room there for as long as required, and it was there we were to meet our other government contact the next morning. We stayed there for the next four nights sleeping on military cots in an open bay room, and sharing the room with six to eight other soldiers and contractors.

The next morning we met a U.S Army Major and some other contractors who were there to assist in the mission. The next stop in our mission was the Baton Rouge Civic Center to talk to the Louisiana State National Guard authorities, as well as soldiers from the 49th Movement Control Battalion (MCB), a part of 13th SC (E) from Fort Hood, TX. The Civic Center was transformed into office areas with prefabricated walls and cubical areas for conferences and working groups sustaining federal, state, local government agencies as well as Non-Governmental Organizations (NGOs). We talked with the Louisiana State Officials, and soldiers from the 49th MCB who told us that they were setting up a command cell there at the Civic Center and that their commander was located at the New Orleans Airport at their higher headquarters location. Their commander was receiving a mission brief on the future support operations. We decided that the New Orleans Airport was the place to be if we were to get our marching orders, so south toward the New Orleans Airport we went. The traffic going south on Interstate-10 was bumper to bumper. It should have only been a thirty or forty minute drive from Baton Rouge to New Orleans, but on this particular occasion, it took us two hours. Upon arriving at the airport and finding the 13th SC (E) headquarters, we checked in though security and were escorted to the tent where the personnel we needed to talk to were located. After saying our greetings, we sat down in front of a map and an easel of paper, where a senior non-commissioned officer (NCO) briefed the situation, projected mission, shortfalls, and how we could help. We listened to the brief and reviewed maps of the local area pertaining to road network and projected forward distribution points. The main reasons for these decisions were: to identify some sort of network or distribution routes from Federal Emergency Management Agency (FEMA) to the State of Louisiana authorities to facilitate a smooth commodity transition or hand-off. Visibility of supply movement would be required in order to make this concept work. This procedure is called In-Transit Visibility (ITV). The key is to determine the proper placement of interrogators for Radio Frequency Identification Devices (RFID) monitoring.

Scope of Work

The concept was for BCS3 to track commodities including emergency supplies such as water, medical materials, and food, in near-real time, flowing in and out of the region. We were to provide visibility and information to facilitate the hand-off of commodities and their movement from FEMA to the State and local agencies. The idea was to establish an automation network consisting of fixed and mobile interrogators to monitor Radio Frequency Identification Devices (RFID) or Tags, on a map-based computer laptop screen through live tracking tools and in-transit visibility. BCS3 would also bring convoy management to the relief efforts providing the capability to see and track the vehicles as they move throughout the region. We set proximity alerts to ensure visibility of vehicles along their path to make sure they make it to their correct destination on time.

Our main purpose was to establish initial contact and assess the mission scope. The task as spelled out by the State of Louisiana officials was to provide a "visibility tool" to assist relief workers to obtain and maintain visibility of supplies as they moved through the state to distribution sites. The mission required five BCS3 systems at various locations throughout the state. In addition, there were four Field System Controller's deployed to work with and train the 13th SC (E) soldiers at each location on BCS3 functionality. There were initially four sites and an additional fifth was added:
- EOC at Baton Rouge

Logistics in Support of Disaster Relief

- Distribution site at Hammond
- 13th SC (E) Headquarters, at the New Orleans Airport
- Distribution site at Alexandria
- A fifth site was established after Hurricane Rita to assist in that region of the State of Louisiana and it was located at Lake Charles

To accomplish the mission, each location required the following equipment:

- Satellite Communications
- RF tags and
- Interrogators
- BCS3

The combination of these systems to accomplish their mission/purpose demonstrates the dependency on our automated systems have on one another, as well as other technology.

Support Concept

The support concept consisted of developing a movement network with all the enablers required, as well as the basic relief supplies. The supplies were to arrive by truck at Alexandria, LA. In addition, Radio Frequency Identification Devises (RIFD) were prepared in advance with one of the five contents:

- Ice
- Water
- Meals Ready to Eat
- Cots
- Tarps
- Miscellaneous

We placed interrogators at each distribution site to read/identify RFID tags. RFID tags were installed on trucks as they left Alexandria. Those RFID tags provided visibility within BCS3 as they arrived at the various distribution sites in the state.

This is the basic overview of the support provided the State of Louisiana and the U.S Army as it related to the Hurricane Katrina

James H. Henderson

efforts. In the following Chapters, the ideas and concepts that have been discussed are elaborated on in more detail.

CHAPTER 2

Framework and Structure

President Dwight D. Eisenhower

President Franklin D. Roosevelt, in the late 1930's, showed an interest in developing a road network of freeways and expressways to link the United States. Congress established The Federal-Aid Highway Act of 1938 to study the feasibility of the development of a statewide highway system. World War II put this initiative on hold for an extended period.

By the time, President Dwight D. Eisenhower became the new commander and chief he had two experiences that helped establish his ideas and concepts in the development of the National System of Interstate and Defense Highways.

In the summer of 1919, the U.S. Army conducted its first transcontinental motor convoy from Washington, D.C. to San Francisco. The operation took sixty-two days to complete and it demonstrated the need for a more durable and reliable road infrastructure.

As the Allied Forces made their push into Germany toward the end of World War II, General Dwight David Eisenhower was in awe with the stability and strength of Germany's autobahn network. Hitler had designed the autobahn network to work in conjunction with the railroad and canal systems to provide him the capability to rapidly move military personnel and equipment across the country. As the Allied Forces fought their way into Germany, General Eisenhower experienced first hand the enhanced mobility the autobahn network provided his forces.

Once Eisenhower became President in 1953, he implemented his ideas of constructing a system of interstate highways across the United States. Also in the 1950's, the country was concerned with nuclear conflict with the Soviet Union, and this modern interstate highway system could provide a means for evacuation and disaster relief support, as well as to allow a quick way to move military personnel and equipment across the nation.

Interstate Highway System

The Dwight D. Eisenhower National System of Interstate and Defense Highways, or as most people call it the Interstate Highway System, is an integrated system of freeways or expressways linking American regions. This network of highways is a system within a system consisting of individual State Interstate Highway Systems coming together to create the larger National Highway System. As of Fiscal Year 2004, the complete system had a total length of 46,837 miles (75,376 km). The Interstate Highways receive federal funding, but the State's must comply with federal standards. Nevertheless, from the beginning of development the states build, operate and ultimately own the system located in their state. The only exception is the federally owned Woodrow Wilson Bridge on the Capital Beltway (I-95/I-495). Construction and maintenance continues on the Interstate Highway system, but the federal government officially concluded development in 1991. Estimated cost of the highway system was $25 billion over a twelve-year period. When it was all said and done the ending costs were $114 billion over a thirty-five year period.

The Interstate numbering system consists of one, two, and three-digit signs. One and two-digit signs displaying even numbers are east-west routes and odd numbers are north-south routes. Three-digit signs displaying the first digit even are routes through or around cities, and signs displaying the first digit odd are spurs into cities. States determine speed limits ranging from 65 to 80 mph (100 to 130 km/h) in rural areas and in urban areas; limits are strictly regulated between 50 to 65 mph (80 to 100 km/h). The following is an example of the United States Interstate System (See Figure 1).

Logistics in Support of Disaster Relief

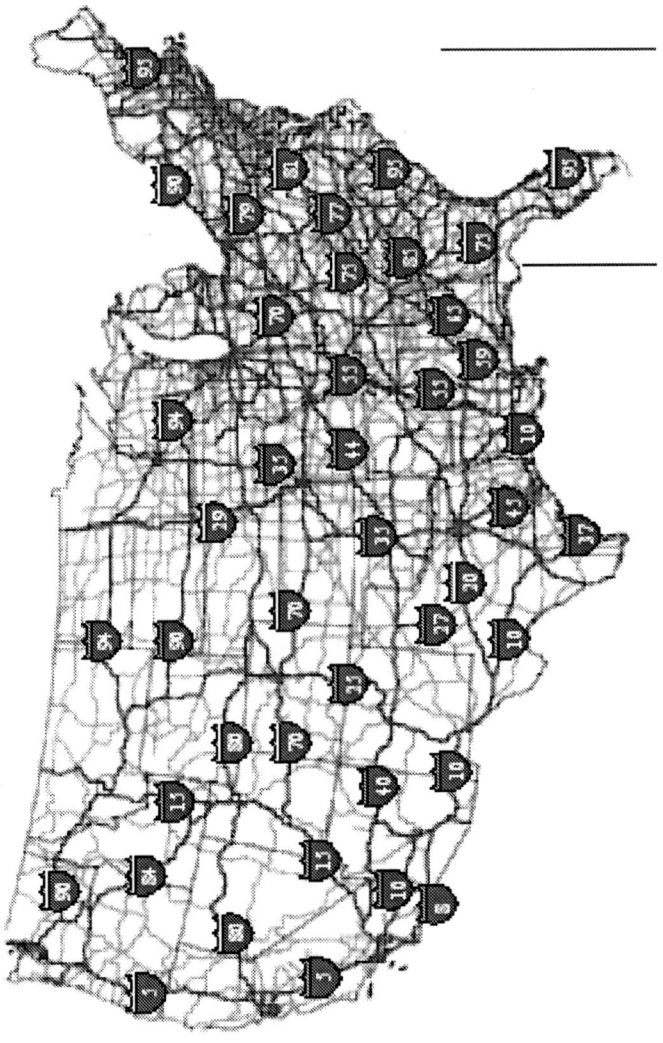

Figure 1, United States Interstate System

Duel Usage

Besides automobile travel and commercial usage, the interstate highways have a dual usage in their development to support military and civil defense operations. This dual purpose is ideal for emergency city evacuation in the event of a nuclear war or a natural disaster like earthquakes and hurricanes. One concept used by many states is to reverse the flow of traffic on one side so that all lanes become outbound lanes. The idea called Contraflow was used in limited operations in support of hurricanes Charley, Katrina, and Rita. Contraflow lane reversal changes the flow of traffic from its original intent. An example is for incoming highway lanes changed to outbound lanes maximizing the number of lanes available to support an emergency evacuation of an area. Contraflow lane reversal is used for emergency measures only and must be coordinated prior to implementation, as well as properly controlled and monitored to maintain an orderly traffic flow in the direction required. Control points are required to assist in the lane management reversal to control on and off ramps at interchanges. It also assists in the regulation of traffic flow at network choke points. These control or checkpoints are man intensive, but with the proper enablers (communications and automation) coordinated and established early in the operations these requirements can be multi-tasked to provide visibility along the road network to show flow. Remember logistics supports security operations because without logistical relief's support to the disaster victims, the situation could escalate to where the victims themselves take matters into their own hands leading to confusion, violence, and looting. An example of this is road rage due to lane congestion and slow evacuation procedures of a region. In addition, lack of information could lead to confusion in the evacuation route, as well as looting of local business as victims try to solve their own situation. Enables and their usage are discussed in *Chapter 10, Building the Relief Support Network*

Another theory developed in the original design of the interstate highway network is the corridors of circulation concept, which was designed to establish corridors to link metropolitan areas to facilitate the evacuation of large urban areas. Other corridors have been added since the original concept, but the basic requirement was assemble. Lanes were established in the direction of longitudinal and latitudinal corridors across the United States. An example of these high traffic lanes are interstate highways I-5, I-15, I-40, I-55, I-70, I-95). The following diagram depicts these corridors of circulation in Figure 2, United States Interstate Corridors, and North to South, and East to West.

Logistics in Support of Disaster Relief

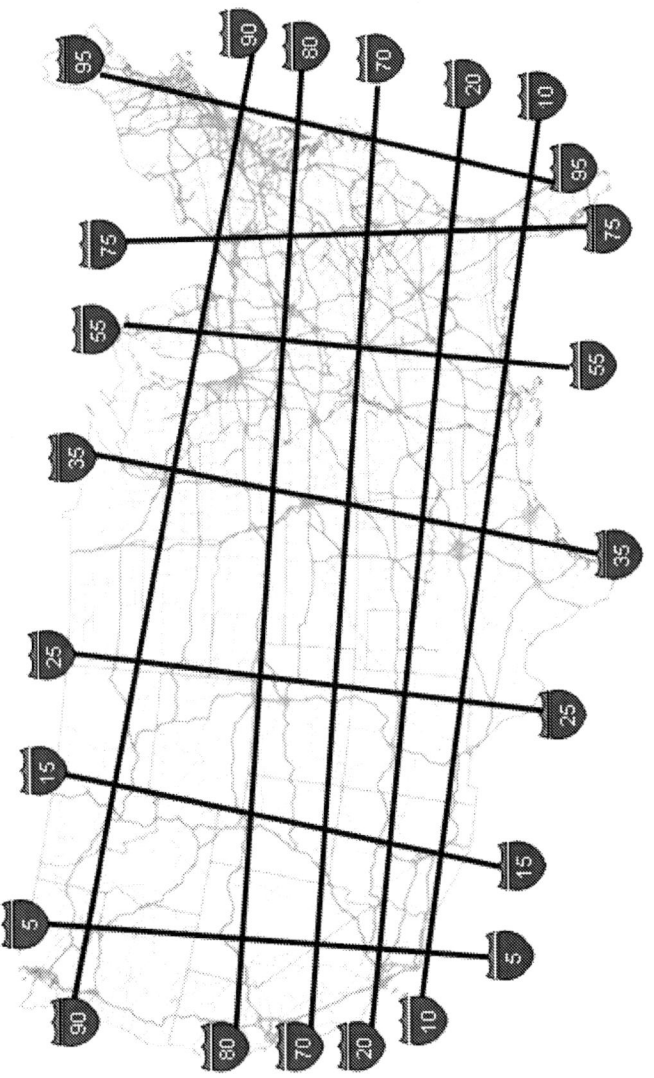

Figure 2, United States Interstate Corridors, North to South and East to West

CHAPTER 3

The Plan

Planning

There are many types of plan concepts. There are financial plans, house plans, strategic plans, vacation plans, just to name a few. Whatever the reason to develop a plan, there is one constant point and that is to make something happen. No matter who you are, or what you do, everyone conducts some sort of planning throughout our day-to-day life. How well we perform the development is the key to building an executable plan with a successful outcome.

Decision-Making

Decision-making when done correctly can provide the answer to difficult problems, issues, and/or situations. There are many forms of the decision-making process used throughout the world, but I will discuss only three, the *Basic Problem Solving Model*, the *Military Decision Making Process (MDMP)*, and *Staff Estimates*. When implementing either process you must remember that the decision-making process needs formalization. Staff agencies, local and state government organizations frequently change personnel leading to a lack of continuity within the staff structure. By identifying a common framework to conduct planning and decision-making under, you have laid the foundation that facilitates the integration of new personnel and provides the capability to add organizations even as the process is in progress without causing set backs or turmoil.

Basic Problem Solving Model

To conduct simple decision-making the best procedure is the Basic Problem Solving Model.

Basic Problem Solving Model

1. Identify the Problem
2. Develop Solutions
3. Compare Alternatives
4. Decision

This procedure has four straightforward elements. The first is to *"Identify the Problem"* this is not as easy as it may seem. What looks like the problem may only be the face value and sometimes what appears to be the problem is only one of many issues. Until you identify all the issues, do you really see the problem to resolve? The second is to *"Develop Solutions"* where you extend options or alternative that provide answers that might solve the problem. This is the most important phase of the model in that during this phase of the process you begin to develop courses of action that could give a solution to the problem. The third element is to *"Compare Alternatives"* this is the process of calculating approximately the alternatives. At this phase of the procedure, all options are evaluated against subjective criteria and ranked to determine their relevance. The fourth is self-explanatory; it is the *"Decision"* that is made after all the above is completed. So now, let us provide an example of the process in use, the problem – *"there is no electricity after the storm to power your house."* I will demonstrate the Basic Problem Solving Model:

1. Identify the Problem – I need a generator
2. Develop Solutions - what are my options,
    - Make / Model
    - Gas / Diesel
    - Horsepower
    - Mobile / Stationary
3. Compare Alternatives - cost, size, reliability, etc.
4. Decision – Colman 8 hp, gasoline, mobile

The process just explained is good for uncomplicated problems and issues, but for scenarios that are more complex, we need to use a process

Logistics in Support of Disaster Relief

that allows for more analysis and estimates that identify all the problems, and collects the issues for resolution. Here is an example of what I am discussing. The problem is *"10,000 to 20,000 individuals are homeless due to a hurricane."* The problem is big enough just to find shelter for the individuals, but there are added issues associated with the problem that complicate the situation even more like electricity, water, food, cots, blankets, and heat, fans, or air conditioning just to name a few. The additional issues that complicate the problem are *specified, implied, and essential tasks*, and they need solving along with the problem, or they to will become problems. Specified tasks you are directed to do. Implied tasks you must do, but are not necessarily directed to do, and Essential tasks must be accomplished or risk failure. Remember essential tasks can align under either specified or implied tasks. The following is an example if you tried to use the Basic Problem Solving Model:

1. **Identify the Problem** – 10,000 to 20,000 individuals are homeless due to a hurricane

2. **Develop Solutions** - what are my options
   a. **Options**,
      1) Federal Emergency Management Agency (FEMA)
      2) Red Cross
      3) Local and State Agencies
      4) Military
      5) Non-Government Agencies
      6) Combination of any or all of the above

   b. **Additional Questions**,
      1) What is the extent of damage to the surrounding area?
      2) What are the number of facilities or structures that can house, between 500 and 1,000 persons and are still in existence within the local area?
      3) Do these existing structures have electricity?
      4) Is there running water?
      5) What other supplies are required?

   c. **Tasks**,
      1) **Specified**: Find Shelter for 10,000 to 20,000 individuals

    a) **Essential**: Extent of damage to the surrounding area
    b) **Essential**: Number of facilities or structures existing
2) **Implied**:
    a) **Implied**: Provide electricity
      (1) Generators
      (2) Wiring
      (3) Electricians
    b) **Implied**: Provide running water
      (1) Toilettes
      (2) Washbasins
      (3) Showers
      (4) Equipment
        (a) **Essential**: Toilet Paper
        (b) **Essential:** Wash Towels
        (c) **Essential:** Shower Towels
        (d) **Essential:** Shower Shoes
        (e) **Essential:** Hygiene
      (5) Maintenance and Sanitation
    c) **Implied:** Environmental Control
      (1) Air Circulation
      (2) Fans
      (3) Heating Units
      (4) Air Conditioning Units
    d) **Implied:** Provide Food
      (1) Type (Cold or Hot)
      (2) Eating Areas
        (a) **Essential:** Tables and Chairs
        (b) **Essential:** Utensils
      (3) Cooking Facilities
        (a) **Essential:** Cooks
        (b) **Essential:** Cooking Equipment
        (c) **Essential:** Cooking Utensils
      e) **Implied:** Sleeping Comforts
    (1) Cots
    (2) Blankets
  f) **Implied:** Medical Support
    (1) Doctors
    (2) Facilitates

(3) Equipment
   (4) Supplies
1) **Compare Alternatives** – Dilemma is the list of Issues (Contingency Circumstances) – Implied Tasks are as big and overwhelming as the original Problem – Specified Task.

Problem – Specified Tasks	Issues (Contingency Circumstances) – Implied Tasks
Find shelters	Provide electricity
	Provide running water
	Environmental control
	Provide food
	Sleeping comforts
	Medical Support

Answer: You must develop a process that can solve the immediate Specified Task, as well as capture and work the list of Implied Tasks. The Basic Problem Solving Model is not designed to handle complex problems.

2) **Decision** – "**No decision made**"? Find a way to get the Implied Tasks worked separately, by technical people, while the overall Specified Task is worked.

Therefore, to handle the complex problems and issues that are associated with disaster relief support operations we will require a more in depth process.

Military Decision Making Process and Staff Estimate

The military does the best job with planning of any organization I know. They have training courses designed just to instruct leaders in the art of decision-making, and this training taught is the Military Decision Making Process (MDMP) and Staff Estimates. The process educates their leaders in decision-making and Course of Action (COA) development. Utilizing the process, they construct complex plans to synchronize multiple units in the execution of a phased combat operation, as well as contingency plans. It has often been said, "That the Army had future operations staffs concerned only with the question *"What If"*, and their only purpose in life is to build contingency plans." I do not know if this is true, but the philosophy is what we need to propagate as we begin to research and develop disaster relief support plans. This is because these plans have to lay out courses of action and contingence plans that provide different options to a scenario that is very uncertain in outcome and destruction. The plan has to be so complete that no matter the devastation there are always options described in detail for local and state agencies to coordinate and synchronize so that the execution is almost automatic in nature. Let us review this procedure called the Military Decision Making Process (MDMP) and Staff Estimates.

- **Military Decision Making Process (MDMP)** - is a standard planning decision-making model. Key components of MDMP are:
  - Receive mission
  - Mission analysis
  - Course of Action development
  - COA Analysis
  - COA Comparison
  - COA Approval
  - Orders Production

- **Estimates** - are formal processes used to analyze a problem from a specific functional area, providing an in depth staff analysis of the situation. There are two types of estimates, and the reason for the two different estimates is the time given to provide a solution or at least start some sort of action to give time for further analysis.

- **Commander's Estimate** provides for a broader outlook on the situation, by conducting a general analysis of a problem, rather than a detailed analysis. The Commander's Estimate offers an autonomous

Logistics in Support of Disaster Relief

analysis of a problem and in turn a quicker solution to start to implement.

- **Staff Estimate** is a modified problem analysis method geared to specific staff agencies or a particular functional area of expertise. The Staff Estimate guarantees that all aspects of problem and its related issues are analyzed in detail so follow on staff coordination and synchronization can happen.   Staff agency examples:
  - Operations
  - Logistics
  - Medical
  - Maintenance
  - Transportation
  - Sanitation
  - Etc.

To provide for the limited time factor required to begin execution, as well as to conduct detailed analysis needed to develop a complete plan the incorporation of both procedures is required. To achieve the proper outcome and solution the two processes are equally supportive to one another in they provide for a quick execution of some tasks (Specified Tasks), while other staff agencies are conducting detail analysis of other tasks, as well as lead to additional planning, coordination, synchronization, and execution related to specific functional areas (Implied Tasks). So let us review the seven components of the Military Decision Making Process (MDMP).

- **Receive Mission** – is normally self-explanatory, but the bottom line is something has happened and some sort of reaction is required *"Who, What, When, Where, Why, and How,"* are all part of the problem to be resolved. Therefore, an initial assessment must be conducted by the staff or other agencies involved, consisting of staff estimates, to prepare for Mission Analysis.

- **Mission analysis** – accurately defines the problem *"Who, What, When, Where, Why, and How,"* needing to be resolved. At times, the problem statement is easily recognized, but other times it is very hard to understand. One objective is that the mission statement provides

organizational focus. The key to a good Mission Analysis is a clearly defined mission statement. The following are important steps of the Mission Analysis process:
- Analyze available documentation
- Operations Orders
- Standard Operating Procedures (SOPs)
- Verbal guidance
- Polices
- Regulations
- Any other relevant documents
- Maps / Terrain
- Determine: specified / implied / essential tasks
- Review available assets
- Determine constraints
- Identify critical facts and assumptions
- Determine initial recon requirements
- Plan use of available time
- Develop restated mission
- Conduct mission analysis brief
- Approve restated mission
- Develop initial, proposed intent
- Issue guidance
- Issue warning order
- Review facts / assumptions

- **Course of Action (COA) development** – identifies acceptable options that if implemented accomplish the mission or resolve the problem. Each COA considered must be suitable (can accomplish mission), feasible (within capabilities of organization, agencies, or commercial venders), acceptable (means justify the ends), distinguishable (each COA must distinctly different from others), and have completeness (an inclusive review of all options). The following are steps to develop COAs:
    - Analyze relative capabilities
    - Create options
    - Identify organization, agencies, or commercial venders
    - Develop scheme of execution

- Assign organization / agencies / commercial venders
- Prepare COA statements / diagrams

- **COA Analysis** – is the implementation of a detailed study of each COA. This procedure analyzes all the data provided and organizes it in such away that the results provide you the ability to compare each COA. The following are steps to COA Analysis:
  - Assemble the tools
  - Maps/pictures/terrain analysis products
  - COA diagrams
  - Synchronization Matrixes
  - Event Templates
  - Staff estimates
  - List all organization, agencies, or commercial venders
  - List assumptions
  - Are they still valid, and relevant
  - Need to make any additional assumptions
  - Have any new information that validates existing assumptions
  - List know critical events and decision points
  - Critical events are actions you know or anticipate occurring that warrant detailed analysis
  - Decision Points are actions you know or anticipate that may require a significant decision
  - Determine evaluation criteria
  - What criteria to analyze and compare each COA
  - How to quantify each criterion
  - Select war-game method
  - Belt technique - analyzes and synchronizes all activities in a given area, very time consuming
  - Box technique - analyzes all activities in a selected area, very detailed and focused, and a good technique in time-constrained environment. This technique prioritizes events down to just a few to evaluate, and ignores other events to then be reviewed at another time

- Avenues in depth - analyze all activities from start to finish along a given path. This procedure is very detailed and time consuming
- Select method to record and display results
- Synchronization Matrix – develops a planning tool that you will require later to assist in coordination and rehearsals. This procedure is a detailed synchronization of events and is time consuming
- Sketch note method is faster; less detailed, and development of a synchronization matrix is required later
- War-game actions and assess results
- Must be realistic
- Action and counter-action
- Remain unbiased
- List advantages and disadvantages (as found)
- Continually assess COA feasibility, acceptability, and suitability
- Avoid drawing premature conclusions and gathering facts to support such conclusions
- Compare COAs during comparison process: "Not during war game"

- **COA Comparison** – determines decision criteria and assigns weighting values to criteria
    - Be as objective as possible
    - Assess Risk
    - Make recommendation

- **COA Approval** – upon completion of COAs development, evaluation, and staff has come to a recommendation, they then conduct a decision brief laying out the plan
    - Select COA
    - Assess Risk
    - Specify Type of Order

- **Orders Production** – publication of written order and guidance in the form of a document plan and it is then sent out to all players involved

- Translate into Plan / Order
- Incorporate Branches and Sequels
- Establish Control Measures
- Synchronize Plan / Order

The last phase of the process is conducting a good rehearsal so all players both understand and can execute their portion of the plan. There are five types of rehearsal the Confirmation Brief, Back Brief, Operational Events Rehearsal, Support Rehearsal, Task or Standard Operating Procedure (SOP) Rehearsal. The two that are most important in my opinion are the Operational Events and the Support Rehearsals, because they bring all the plays to the table that facilitates coordination and synchronization. When operating in a constrained planning time environment the outcome is usually when you need more time or information and you get less, and when you need less information and involvement you tend to get more.

Planning in Time Constrained Environment	Require	Acquire
Available Planning Time	More	Less
Level of Supervisor Involvement	Less	More
Detail in Supervisor Guidance	Less	More
Flexibly and Latitude of Staff	More	Less
Number of COA Developed	More	Less
Detailed Operations Order to Publish	More	Less

The above table is usually the norm of most planning situations. Practice and understanding of the decision-making process can drastically reduce planning time.

So now, let us work the above problem utilizing the Military Decision Making Process (MDMP) and Staff Estimates.

1. **Receive mission** - 10,000 to 20,000 individuals are homeless due to a hurricane

2. **Mission analysis** - "Who, What, When, Where, Why, and How", and clearly define mission statement,

Restated Mission Statement:

As of 112130JUL07, Hurricane Fred has damaged the southern gulf coastline and 10,000 to 20,000 individuals are homeless. On order, Federal, State, and Local government agencies, as well as Non-government Organizations (NGOs), and commercial venders, provide support in the areas of personnel, equipment, supplies, and services as described and directed in this operations plan and supported by presidential decree, and/or contracts.

3. **Course of Action development** - options,
    1) Federal Emergency Management Agency (FEMA)
    2) Red Cross
    3) Local and State Agencies
    4) Military
    5) Non-Government Agencies
    6) Combination of any or all of the above

4. **COA Analysis** - analyzes data and organizes,

Conduct Cdr Estimate	Conduct Staff Estimate
⬇	⬇
Problem – Specified Tasks	Issues (Contingency Circumstances) – Implied Tasks
⬇	⬇
Find Shelters	Provide electricity
	Provide running water
	Environmental Control
	Provide Food
	Sleeping Comforts
	Medical Support

Logistics in Support of Disaster Relief

5. **COA Comparison** – assign criteria and values,

COA #s	Flexibility	Simplicity	Capability	C2	Totals
1) Federal Emergency Management Agency (FEMA)	1	2	2	1	6
2) Red Cross	1	2	3	1	7
3) Local and State Agencies	1	1	1	2	5
4) Military	1	1	1	3	6
5) Non-Government Agencies	1	2	2	1	6
6) Combination of any or all of the above	2	3	4	4	13

6. **COA Approval** - make recommendation, COA #6 - Combination of any or all of the above
7. **Orders Production** - publication of written order and guidance in the form of a document plan, and sent out to all players involved.

The above is a simple depiction of the procedures required to accomplish a complex problem, in reality it would take a lot more time and staff involvement to complete a plan that would support a problem of this magnitude. I hope that this gets the point across and generates thoughts and beginnings to formulate ideas on how to conduct such a process.

James H. Henderson

Bands of Support

    The next item I will cover is a planning concept that may already be in place in certain parts of the United States, but may not be to the extent that I am going to discuss. I call this concept the *Bands of Support* principal, which requires local and state government officials to develop agreements between different regions or areas of the state, which will provide support during disaster relief operations. Remember this is just an example for planning purposes, if an area is already doing something to this effect then good for them, but if not then this provides an idea of how thinking "out of the box" can facilitate course of action development. A good example of this concept in my home town immediately after Katrina is the local power company, the trucks and personnel supporting my area were not my local company, but from South Carolina. Another example was the local police department who also had support from another state. Bottom line is they had developed co-op agreements, in the power company case between the different firm or firms, and in the police department it could have been between the local cities or a state agreement, whichever the situation, the concept works. So now, let us talk through this idea as if we were executing MDMP performing steps; receive mission, mission analysis, course of action development and course of action analysis. We are going to review the process from the local government's area of control thru to the state government's regional control, and look at some different thoughts.

    The local government of course has its own assets to utilize in support of debris removal of city and county roads and streets. However, in a disaster we would not know to what extent the damage could occur, and the city and county equipment may be damaged or destroyed. This leads to the idea that if there are local businesses in the area that could support debris removal then the city or county officials should put in place an agreement or contract to augment the local city or county assets as required. This could be as simple as an written agreement, between the local business and the city or county, which allows for the usage of personnel and equipment to support the city or county, in the case of a disaster relief operation. When the business supports the city or county will could pay all fuel cost and the business could agree to donate the personnel time and equipment utilized in support of the community for a set period. An example of this idea is in the small town north of my home. There are timber and gravel companies, the timber company has cutting, loading, and hauling equipment designed for large tree and debris removal, and the gravel company has a variety of vehicles that can haul debris, as well as move dirt and gravel to repair roads and streets. I understand that FEMA will pay for this type of assistance, but it takes some time for them to assemble in an area and begin contracting for support. This is the immediate support required immediately after a disaster has occurred, and once FEMA and other federal agencies move in then they can take over these agreements and turn them in the support contracts applying funding to augment these businesses in their work costs, which is great in that it puts dollars back into the disaster community. The key is the immediate support these agreements can provide to a local community, as well as already having a base for FEMA to fall in on and continue recovery operations. And if the state government would take the state and break it up into regional bands consisting of these local government area agreements they could develop bands of support where if one band is hit another regional band could be alerted and begin support immediately until the disaster area or another agencies can take over operations. Looking at the below diagram (See Figure 3, Band of Support) the example state is broken up into three (3) regional bands of support. In each regional band of support, the local cities and counties have developed support agreements with local business to assist in disaster relief operation as required. In the event of a disaster in band one (1); the individual local city or county area agreement could begin to support that area, a different regional band like band two (2), or a even a combination of bands two (2) and three (3) could provide support depending on the magnitude of the disaster. Nevertheless, support would get to the area quicker and relief operation could begin only hours after a disaster have occurred.

James H. Henderson

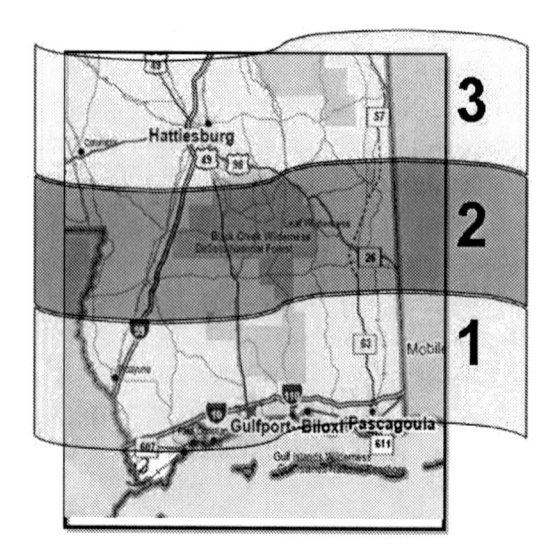

Figure 3, Bands of Support

Now that we have talked through this idea, we are now ready to put thoughts down on paper and provide an example of performing steps; receive mission, mission analysis, course of action development, and course of action analysis to this concept.

1. **Receive mission** – Local cities and counties need augmentation support in debris removal due to a disaster, until federal agencies can react.
2. **Mission analysis** - "Who, What, When, Where, Why, and How" and clearly define the mission statement.

Restated Mission Statement:

As of 112130JUL07, Hurricane Fred has damaged the southern gulf coastline twenty (20) local cities and five (5) counties need augmentation support in debris removal until what time federal agencies can react. On order State and Local government agencies, as well as Non-government Organizations (NGOs), and commercial venders as designated provide support in the areas of personnel, equipment, supplies, and services as described and directed in this operations plan and supported by agreements, and/or contracts.

3. **Course of Action development** - options, and for this exercise, we will work one (1) COA, that being *"Band of Support"*.

COA #1, Band of Support

4. **COA Analysis** - analyzes data and organizes,

Conduct Cdr Estimate	Conduct Staff Estimate	Conduct Staff Estimate
⬇	⬇	⬇
Specified Tasks	**Implied Tasks**	**Essential Tasks**
⬇	⬇	⬇
Develop State Regional Bands of Support	Cities Create Local Businesses Area Agreements	City Develop Agreements with Timber Company
Organize City Area Agreements into State Regional Bands of Support	Counties Create Local Businesses Area Agreements	County Develop Agreements with Timber Company
Organize County Area Agreements into State Regional Bands of Support	Cities Develop Implementation Plan to Active Support	City Develop Agreements with Gravel Company
Develop State Wide Implementation Plan to active Support	Counties Develop Implementation Plan to Active Support	County Develop Agreements with Gravel Company

As stated, this is a simple example of the first four steps utilizing MDMP. Remember this was just an example to get you thinking how to get started, in fact to develop COAs that accomplish a complex problem it would take a great deal of time and considerable staff involvement.

Military Capability

Our armed forces can provide a wealth of resources to almost every situation. Understand that these assets will require activation by either state or federal government officials; but that state and local officials need to be aware of the type of equipment and services the National Guard, Reserve, or Active Duty forces can bring to the table. Military staff organizations are built around administrative command and control (C2) to assist in the daily operations of mission completion, as well as support. They train and have the capability to react at a moments notice. These organizations can provide logistical support in the areas of medical, supply, transportation, and even engineer support, to name just a few. For local and state planners to develop an executable plan they must recognize the capabilities the military can provide so they can utilize the resources to their maximum potential. The following are generic examples of military units and organizations. The Army's new transformation plan for our military force structure may change these organizations in the number of personal or equipment, but for planning proposes these depictions of unit specialties and capabilities and of equipment and services, will suffice.

Medical

Medical staffs - can provide command and control in the areas of administrative support and technically supervision of medical units assigned. Capabilities include:
1. Command and control all medical units in its area of operations (AO).
2. Provide staff functions in managing medical assets to meet patient workload demand.
3. Offer staff expertise in medical operations that can advise senior leaders and officials on medical requirements, and provide solutions and alternatives to the disaster area medical situation.
4. The organization provides medical staff capability for directive of patient movements from the very start of treatment, as well as between medical treatment facilities.

Logistics in Support of Disaster Relief

Forward Surgical Team (FST) - offers a rapidly deployable, urgent surgical capability to patients who cannot withstand further evacuation. The FST is capable of continuous operations for up to 72-hours without resupply, and provides vital, initial surgery for patients unable for transport to a standard treatment facility. Capabilities include:
1. Surgical capability based on two operating room tables with a surgical capacity of 24-hours per day.
2. Emergency medical treatment consists of patient receiving, triage, and pre-op services.
3. With its organic medical equipment, the team can offer initial surgery and postoperative care for up to thirty (30) critically wounded patients over a period of 72-hours.
4. Provide postoperative acute nursing care for up to eight (8) patients.
5. FST equipment (minus vehicles) and personnel can deploy in one aircraft for initial entry, as well as helicopter sling-load operations.

Medical Battalion, Logistics - can provide medical supplies, equipment maintenance, optical fabrication, and blood (processing) storage and distribution. Company's capabilities include:
1. The Battalion has companies that can receive, classify, and issue 200 STON of medical supplies per day.
2. Companies can store up to 686 STON of medical supplies.
3. Units can make available maintenance services in support of medical equipment.
4. Processes, stores, and distributes blood (less frozen blood) to medical units.
5. The battalion and its company have the capability to coordinate with other military staff organizations on the request of transportation assets for delivery of medical supplies, and their redistribution of commodities.
6. Synchronize medical emergency resupply using aviation and ground evacuation assets.
7. The companies can offer two platoons that can operate from two forward support locations.

8. Platoons can receive, classify, and issue 22 STON of medical supplies per day.
9. In addition, the platoons can stores up to 22 STON of medical supplies.

Hospital Unit - offers initial wound surgery, postoperative treatment, or stabilizes and evacuate patients to the higher level of care. Capabilities include:
1. Hospital can provide treatment and housing for up to 296 patients.
2. The hospital offers eight (8) intensive care wards consisting of twelve (12) beds, seven (7) intermediate care wards with twenty (20) beds, two (2) minimal care wards of twenty (20) beds, and one 1 neuropsychiatry care ward consisting of twenty (20) beds.
3. The hospital can provide surgical capability of eight operating room tables supporting up to 144 hours per day.
4. Facilities that can provide consultation services for patients referred from other medical treatment facilities, as well as dental, pharmacy, clinical laboratory, blood banking, radiology, physical therapy, nutrition care, central material service, patient administration, laundry service, and religious support for staff and patients.
5. Each hospital work area is supported with three (3) days of medical supplies and with an additional seven (7) days in reserve.

Medical Air and Ground Ambulance Company's capabilities include:
1. Air Ambulance Company operates 15 UH-60A/Q air ambulances with single-lift capability of sixty (60) litters.
2. Air Ambulance Company provides in flight medical treatment and patient observation.
3. Air Ambulance Company offers internal/external load capability for moving medical personnel, supplies, equipment, and whole blood.

Logistics in Support of Disaster Relief

4. Ground Ambulance Company provides 40 high-mobility multipurpose-wheeled vehicle (HMMWV) ambulances with single-lift capability of 96 litters.
5. Ground Ambulance Company offers relocation of patients between hospitals and other medical treatment and care, as well as provides emergency movement of medical personnel and supplies.

Some of the medical equipment that could be made available for disaster relief support includes:
- Seven (7) truck, forklift (FL), variable reach, 4,000-lb
- Seven (7) truck, FL, rough-terrain (RT), 6,000-lb
- Four (4) truck, FL, RT, 10,000-lb
- Twenty-four (24) box, shipping military-owned demountable container (MILVAN) (8x8x20 ft)
- Thirteen (13) dolly set, lift, transportable, shelter, 7 1/2-ton (M1022)
- Nine (9) generator set, diesel, 100kw, trailer-mounted
- Two (2) laundry unit, trailer-mounted
- Thirteen (13) shelter, tactical, ISU (8x8x20 ft)
- Fifty-nine (59) air conditioner, heater
- Thirty-six (36) tent, extendable, modular, personnel
- Tent, expandable, modular, personnel (TEMPER) (various configurations)
- Four (4) tank, fabric, collapsible, water, 3,000-gallon
- Thirteen (13) truck, cargo, drop-side, 5-ton
- Two (2) truck, FL, RT, 4,000-pound
- Fifteen (15) UH-60A/Q
- Four (4) forward area refueling equipment (FARE)
- Twelve (12) drum, fabric, collapsible, petroleum, oils, and lubricants (POL), 500-gallon
- Forty (40) four-litter M997 high-mobility multipurpose wheeled vehicle (HMMWV) ambulances

James H. Henderson

Supply

Petroleum Pipeline & Terminal Operating Company - manage terminal and pipeline facilities for receiving, storing, and issuing, all types of bulk fuels. Depending on type of storage capability, the unit can store approximately 7,875,000 gallons of bulk petroleum. Some of the fuel handling equipment that may be available for disaster relief support includes:

- Six (6) 10,000-gal collapsible bag (petroleum)
- One (1) forward area refueling equipment (FARE) w/3 500-gal collapsible drums
- One (1) fuel system supply point (FSSP) 60,000-gal (includes six (6) bags listed above, three (3) pumps, and three (3) separators listed below)
- One (1) hose line outfit, 4-in diameter
- Three (3) pump, 350-GPM
- Three (3) filter-separator, 350-GPM

Petroleum Supply Company - can operate a supply point for bulk petroleum products that provides the capability for storage of approximately 2.2 million gallons of fuel, and receive and issue daily up to 1.1 million gallons. Some of the fuel handling equipment that may be available for disaster relief support includes:

- Thirty-six (36) fabric bags 50,000-gal
- Twenty-four (24) fabric bags 20,000-gal
- Twenty-four (24) fabric bags 10,000-gal
- Sixty (60) pump, 350-GPM
- Eighteen (18) drum, collapsible, 500-gal
- Twelve (12) fuel system supply point (FSSP)
- Six (6) forward area refueling equipment (FARE)
- Six (6) hose line outfit, fuel, 4-in diameter

Field Service Company – can provide shower and laundry support. The unit can support up to 18,000 personnel weekly and clean 142,200 pounds of laundry a week.

Supply Company- can receive, store, and issue food, water, fuel, clothing materials, and building supplies. It also has the capability to purify water, and can generate 60,000 gallons of water at three different locations for a total of 180,000 gallons. Some of the water purification and handling equipment that may be available for disaster relief support includes:

- Four (4) forward area water point supply system (FAWPSS)
- Forty (40) tank, collapsible, 3,000-gal, water
- Two (2) fuel system supply point (FSSP), 60,000-gal
- Four (4) tank, collapsible, 3,000-gal, semi trailer-mounted fabric tank (SMFT)
- Four (4) reverse osmosis water purification unit (ROWPU), 3,000-GPH

Mortuary Affairs Collection Company – can operate and maintain twenty (20) collection points and has the capability to conduct searches, to recover, identify, and evacuate remains, as well as to handle change of custody of personal effects and maintain essential records and reports. An average unit can process four hundred (400) remains a day. Important equipment consists of four (4) refrigerated containers assembly, 8x8x20.

Transportation

Light Truck Company – can move supplies and personnel in support over a given area of operations each truck can haul 6 STON of cargo, and 20 passengers (PAX). Some of the transportation assets that may be available include:

- Sixty (60) trucks, 5-ton, drop-side
- Five (5) trucks, cargo, 5-ton

Medium Truck Company - can move bulk or containerized supplies and personnel in support over a given area of operations each truck can haul 15 STON, or ninety (90) 20-ft containers. Some of the transportation assets that maybe available include:

- Sixty (60) trucks, tractor, medium tactical vehicle (MTV), 5-ton, 6x6
- One-Hundred-Fifty (150) semi trailer, M871, 221/2-ton

Medium Truck Company Petroleum (POL) - moves bulk petroleum and can be equipped with either 5,000 or 7,500-gallon tanker trailers. Some of the transportation that may be assets available includes:

- Sixty (60) trucks, tractor, M915, line-haul
- Sixty (60) semi-trailers, tanker, 5,000-gal/7,500-gal

Medium Truck Company (Palletized Loading System) – can move 11 STON a flat-rack and with trailer can haul two (2) flat-racks. Some of the transportation assets that may be available include:

- Four-eight (48) M1075 truck, cargo, heavy, palletized loading system (PLS) transporter
- Four-eight (48) M1076 trailer, palletized, loading, 8x20
- Ninety-six (96) M1077 bed, cargo, demountable, PLS, 8x20

Cargo Transfer Company – is a cargo transfer unit for handling cargo by ship, air, rail, motor, and inland barge terminals. Some of the transportation assets that may be available include:

- Four (4) Truck, tractor, M915
- Four (4) Trailer, 34-ton, M872
- Four (4) rough-terrain forklift (RTFL), 10,000-lb
- Six (6) rough-terrain forklift (RTFL), 4,000-lb
- Two (2) rough terrain (RT), container handler, 50,000-lb

Movement Control Team (MCT) - conducts movement control functions for transporting personnel and materiel. Some of the equipment assets that may be available include:

- One (1) computer, Battle Command Sustainment Support System (BCS3)
- One (1) mobile interrogator reader, hand held

Highway Regulating Team (HRT) – manages highway regulation points, synchronizes traffic movement, and convoy route status. Some of the equipment assets that may be available include:

- One (1) computer, Battle Command Sustainment Support System (BCS3)
- One (1) mobile interrogator reader, hand held

Engineer

Support Company (Field Engineer Unit) – provide horizontal and vertical construction, as well as general road and airfield maintenance and repair. Some of the equipment assets that may be available include:

- One (1) each, Dozer (6/7)
- Three (3) Excavator backhoe, light
- Three (3) Loader Scoop Type: DED 4X4 W/5 CY GP Bucket
- Three (3) Grader Road Motorized: Diesel Driven Heavy
- Three (3) Scraper Earth Moving Self-Propelled: 14-18 CY
- Two (2) Roller Vibratory
- Three (3) Dump Trucks, heavy 10 ton
- Ten (10) Water Purification Set (1500/250 GPM)
- Four (4) Well Drilling Rigs
- Three (3) Power Generation Set
- Four (4) Hand Tool Set (per tradesman)
- One (1) Bailey Bridge Set (100-ft) or equivalent
- Two (2) M2 Rigs, for rafting as required
- Six (6) Semi Trailer Low Bed 40T
- Six (6) Wheel Truck Tractor: MET 8X6 75000 GVW W/W C/S
- Twelve (12) Truck Dump: 20 Ton Diesel Driven 12 CU YD CAP
- Four (4) Truck Tractor: MTV W/E
- Nine (9) Truck Dump: MTV W/E
- Three (3) Crane, 25 Ton

Multi-role Engineer Unit - provide horizontal and vertical construction, and general engineering support. Some of the equipment assets that may be available include:

- Six (6) Dozer (D7/8)
- Nine (9) Excavator Backhoe, light
- Six (6) Excavator Backhoe, heavy
- Three (3) Excavator Trencher
- Three (3) Scoop Loader Type: DED 4X4 W/5 CY GP Bucket
- Nine (9) Grader Road Motorized: Diesel Driven Heavy

- Nine (9) Scrapper Scraper Earth Moving Self-Propelled: 14-18 CY
- Three (3) Roller Vibratory
- Nine (9) Crane, 30 ton
- One (1) Dump Truck, heavy 10 ton
- Twelve (12) Truck, heavy 8 ton cargo w/crane
- Six (6) Concrete Mixers
- Three (3) Quarry Equipment, complete
- Hand Tool Set (per tradesman)
- Bailey Bridge Set, (100 ft) or equivalent
- Three (3) M2 Rigs for rafting as required.
- Three (3) Truck, heavy bridging
- Six (6) Assault Boat
- Six (6) Well Drilling Rigs
- Nine (9) Power Generating Set (medium / heavy)

Synopsis

As stated before, no matter who you are, or what you do everyone conducts some sort of planning, but it is how well we perform the development of that plan that is the key to building an executable plan. The point I wish to restate is there has to be staff investment to develop a workable product. Leadership has to protect the planning cycle so there is the proper time to complete the process.

CHAPTER 4

Operational Control

Information Management

Once the plan is complete, the hardest part then comes into effect, and that is the execution phase. If an organization or agency has prepared itself properly then this may not be a significant emotional event, but if it has not then the staff is in for some long days and nights. Just like in the planning phase, the organization has to clearly recognize how the primary staff and the other agencies will disseminate information and fuse data between its own organization and other agencies to maintain situational awareness, as well as a staff focus and synergy.

This is best handled with the establishment of a *Fusion Cell*, which has it main purpose to correlate, integrate, and distribute data that can provide the organization or other agencies pertinent information that contributes to command and control of the operation. Therefore, the organization must establish a *process* to handle the *input* and *output* of data to facilitate information management. The process identifies the three components in the information management process consisting of the *Organizational Outlook, Organizational Information Flow,* and *Information Flow Elements.*

The first step in creating this process is to design an Organizational Outlook, which lays out the important focal points of the mission and the network and connectivity required. This structural design must be developed from the ground up, aligning the organization and its sub-agencies to establish an architecture that support the process of information management (See Figure 4, Organizational Outlook for Successful Information Management).

Organizational Outlook for Successful Information Management
1. Mission or Operation of the Organization
2. Identify the Agencies or Sub-organizations involved
3. Categorize Expectation for Success
4. Define the Function and Process of each Agency participating: Input/Output
5. Define the Function and Method of each Agency participating: Input/Output
6. Identify Skills/Technology/Tools/Facilities required to conduct the procedure
7. Establish the Connectivity: Data, Voice, Display, Output – Network
8. Recognize and Instruct Specific Training, Techniques, and Procedures (TTP)
9. Refinement of Tools/Connectivity/TTPs to meet Mission expectation

Figure 4, Organizational Outlook for Successful Information Management

After the architecture is laid out and the users have identified the organization's mission, player's expectations, method, resources, and guidance for information management, the next step is to create the Organizational Information Flow diagram. This depicts the task organization of the unit and it's subunits that provide the network to implement procedures for an organizations staff sections and divisions to gather information from its sub-organizations, as well as other agencies and to process the data input and develop data outputs to communicate to higher and subordinate organization and other agencies.

As you can see from Figure 5, Organizational Information Flow, each sub-organization and agencies staff sections information input and output feeds and builds the next level of the overall organizations

Logistics in Support of Disaster Relief

information management structure. The connectivity between the different staff elements, of either automation or voice output, is that established network that connects the staff entities, which supports information flow. To understand what makes up this network and the terminology utilized within the information flow architecture some important definitions need reviewing.

- Input – Consists of written or automated reports and documentation provided from lower to higher, or higher to lower within the organizations.
- Cycle – Is the sequence of events tracked either on an hourly, daily, as required timeline.
- Process – The practice a staff implements which consists of guidelines and procedures to analysis and synthesis in support of information management.
- Personnel – This category identifies those particular staff players with specific duty positions and responsibilities.
- Tool – This is what the network consists of in the area of connectivity voice or automation utilizing computers, phones, servers, network system, etc.
- Responsibility – The organization, agencies, and subunits the outputs expectations pertain to.
- Output: – Consists of written or automated reports, documentation, products, and displays provided from lower to higher, or higher to lower within the organizations.
- Content – Is the fidelity and substance of the input or output provided throughout the organization.
- Format – Guidelines, standard operating procedures (SOP) and other organizational guidance that establishes how to arrange documents, pictures, overlays, as well as live data.
- Means – The way data is displayed and/or stored, examples maybe hard copy, video feed, or network folders.

Once the information has filtered through the organization divisions and staff sections the fusion cell is the final group to evaluate, integrate, and synchronize the data (See Figure 5, Organizational Information Flow).

James H. Henderson

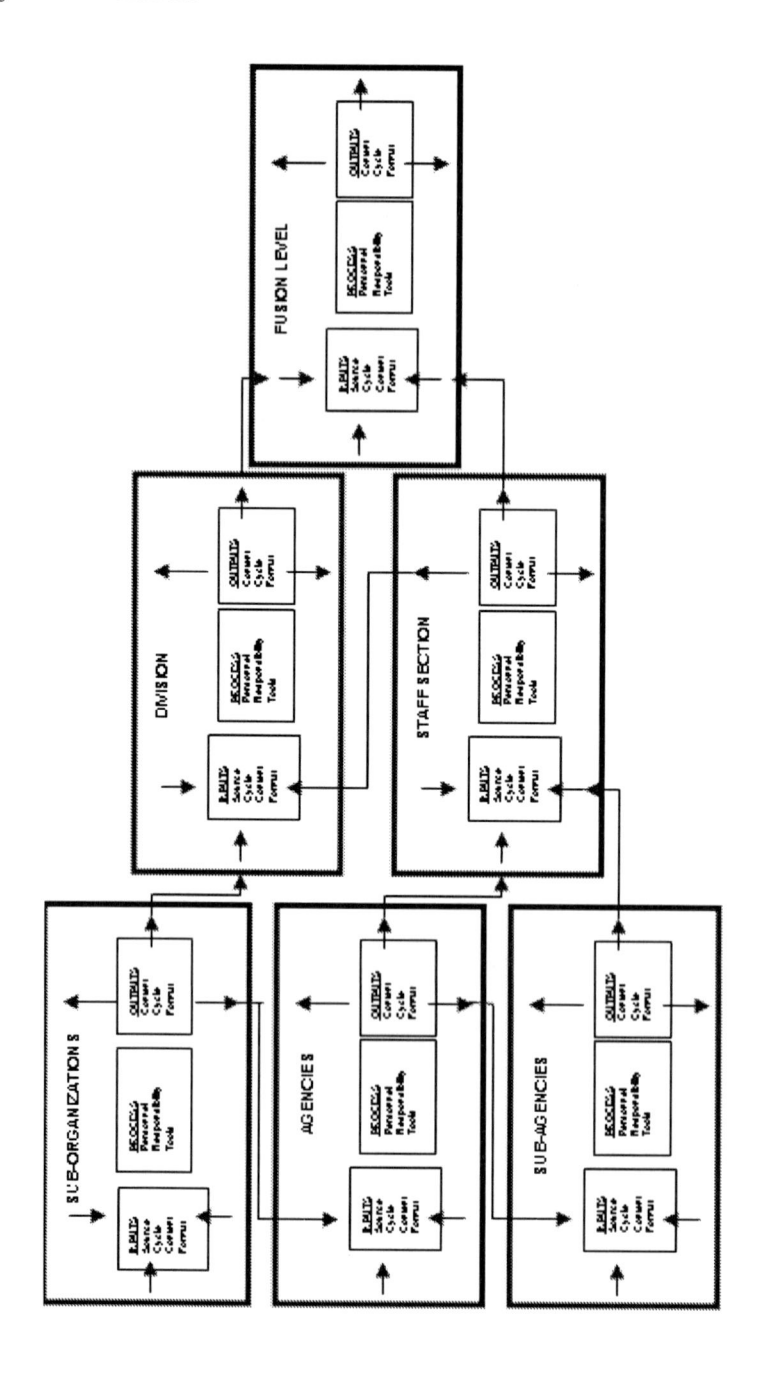

Figure 5, Organizational Information Flow

Logistics in Support of Disaster Relief

The last step in the information management process is to label key elements of the information flow process. As data, input begins to arrive into the process and the first element *"Distribution Means"* is the way that data is shared throughout the organization. The second element is the *"Target"*, which identifies the intent or objective of the mission. The third element is the most important and that is the *"Receipt Validation Agent"*, which confirms and accepts the requirement and channels the request to the right staff section or other agencies. The fourth element is the *"Feedback Loop"* that provides the initial information direction and guidance, by either the command section or other agencies, required to begin staff estimates and analysis. Fifth element *"Source"* recognizes basis of the information and supplies copies of the data by the means it entered the process. The sixth element *"Inject Point"* relates to contribution between staff sections, guidance from command channels, and subordinate sub-organizations and agencies. This interjection of information, guidance, and/or data can be deliberate or incidental, the importance is that this happens before the staff analysis begins, to ensure the most current information trail is gathered. The seventh element *"Analysis"* phase begins where staff sections conduct different forms of problem solving and staff estimates to provide the organization the solution to the issue at hand. Chapter 3, The Plan can assist you in picking the best process to use to provide the best course of action. Last is the eighth element *"Dissemination Agent"* and this is simply the way the organization provides feedback to the sub-organizations and other agencies providing the staff's answer and guidance. The information flow process must be put into place prior to the organization conducting of real world operations so they can practice and train the staff sections, sub-organizations and other agencies in the Organizational Information Flow process (See Figure 6, Information Flow Elements)

Establishing a Mobile Operation Center

In order to establish a mobile operation center or forward response cell you must have the proper equipment and personnel immediately available to operate the center for a 24-hour period, and be able to deploy and setup operational support in a very short timeframe. Last and most important you must be able to sustain these operations until both additional personnel are gathered and deployed to the area, and operations can move to a more stable fixed facility. These initial personnel can setup operations temporally in tents or buildings as long as they have the proper equipment to operate until the time the state and local officials can take over support operations. The following notes are some of the recourses required to establish a workable operation center or response cell that provide capabilities and results:

- Arrange for communications and power generation
- Provide for automation network feeds for computers
- Make available computers, printers, copy machines, etc.
- Supply portable tables, chairs and other furniture
- Make available office supplies (paper, pens, etc.)
- Select an area that not only your organization can setup, but your sub-organizations and other agencies can also establish their staff functions in order to facilitate information flow and coordination.
- Select sites for logistics facilities
- Set up field feeding, billeting, and shower areas
- Evaluate preventive medicine measures to determine specific support requirements (ie potable water)

There are certain elements that assist staff operations and a situational awareness of these areas consist of a knowledge of basic structural design. These elements include the main operations center, separate work cells, and the type of facility used (building or tents). The key to success is an area that facilitates open discussion with briefing capability and areas for staff section, sub-organizations, and other agencies for work areas and breakout sections. The following three figures are provided for review; Figure 7, Example of building and/or tents, Figure 8, Example 1 of a Mobile Operations Center Design, and Figure 9, Example 2 of a Mobile Operations Center Design. The building and tent diagram offers room for a main operations center that is capable of seating forty-four (44) workstations on the main floor and adjacent work cell areas. The workstation furniture can be placed on portable platform risers to give the briefing area an auditorium feel that supports staff visual and communication capabilities. The main idea is to support staff synchronization and synergy within the organization.

Logistics in Support of Disaster Relief

The last step in the information management process is to label key elements of the information flow process. As data, input begins to arrive into the process and the first element "Distribution Means" is the way that data is shared throughout the organization. The second element is the "Target", which identifies the intent or objective of the mission. The third element is the most important and that is the "Receipt Validation Agent", which confirms and accepts the requirement and channels the request to the right staff section or other agencies. The fourth element is the "Feedback Loop" that provides the initial information direction and guidance, by either the command section or other agencies, required to begin staff estimates and analysis. Fifth element "Source" recognizes basis of the information and supplies copies of the data by the means it entered the process. The sixth element "Inject Point" relates to contribution between staff sections, guidance from command channels, and subordinate sub-organizations and agencies. This interjection of information, guidance, and/or data can be deliberate or incidental, the importance is that this happens before the staff analysis begins, to ensure the most current information trail is gathered. The seventh element "Analysis" phase begins where staff sections conduct different forms of problem solving and staff estimates to provide the organization the solution to the issue at hand. Chapter 3, The Plan can assist you in picking the best process to use to provide the best course of action. Last is the eighth element "Dissemination Agent" and this is simply the way the organization provides feedback to the sub-organizations and other agencies providing the staff's answer and guidance. The information flow process must be put into place prior to the organization conducting of real world operations so they can practice and train the staff sections, sub-organizations and other agencies in the Organizational Information Flow process (See Figure 6, Information Flow Elements)

James H. Henderson

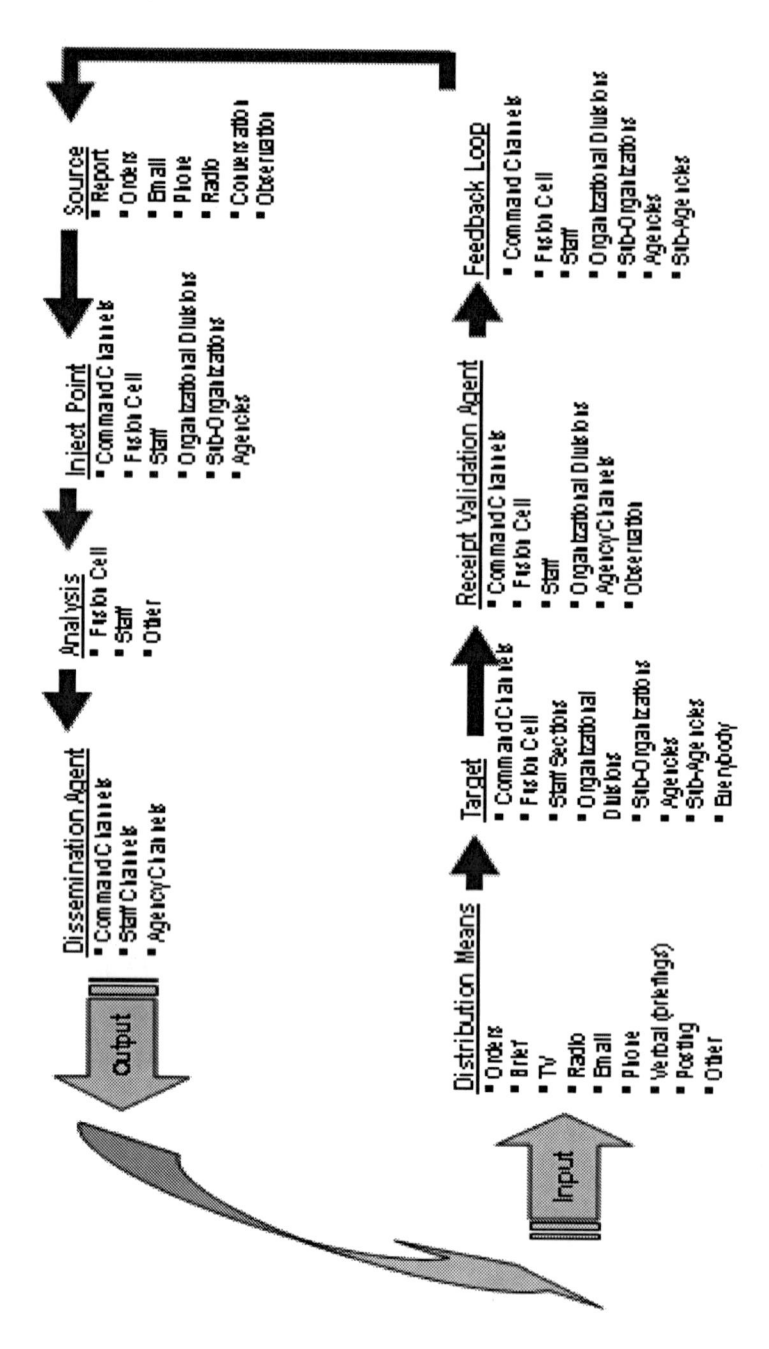

Figure 6, Information Flow Elements

Establishing a Mobile Operation Center

In order to establish a mobile operation center or forward response cell you must have the proper equipment and personnel immediately available to operate the center for a 24-hour period, and be able to deploy and setup operational support in a very short timeframe. Last and most important you must be able to sustain these operations until both additional personnel are gathered and deployed to the area, and operations can move to a more stable fixed facility. These initial personnel can setup operations temporally in tents or buildings as long as they have the proper equipment to operate until the time the state and local officials can take over support operations. The following notes are some of the recourses required to establish a workable operation center or response cell that provide capabilities and results:

- Arrange for communications and power generation
- Provide for automation network feeds for computers
- Make available computers, printers, copy machines, etc.
- Supply portable tables, chairs and other furniture
- Make available office supplies (paper, pens, etc.)
- Select an area that not only your organization can setup, but your sub-organizations and other agencies can also establish their staff functions in order to facilitate information flow and coordination.
- Select sites for logistics facilities
- Set up field feeding, billeting, and shower areas
- Evaluate preventive medicine measures to determine specific support requirements (ie potable water)

There are certain elements that assist staff operations and a situational awareness of these areas consist of a knowledge of basic structural design. These elements include the main operations center, separate work cells, and the type of facility used (building or tents). The key to success is an area that facilitates open discussion with briefing capability and areas for staff section, sub-organizations, and other agencies for work areas and breakout sections. The following three figures are provided for review; Figure 7, Example of building and/or tents, Figure 8, Example 1 of a Mobile Operations Center Design, and Figure 9, Example 2 of a Mobile Operations Center Design. The building and tent diagram offers room for a main operations center that is capable of seating forty-four (44) workstations on the main floor and adjacent work cell areas. The workstation furniture can be placed on portable platform risers to give the briefing area an auditorium feel that supports staff visual and communication capabilities. The main idea is to support staff synchronization and synergy within the organization.

Building

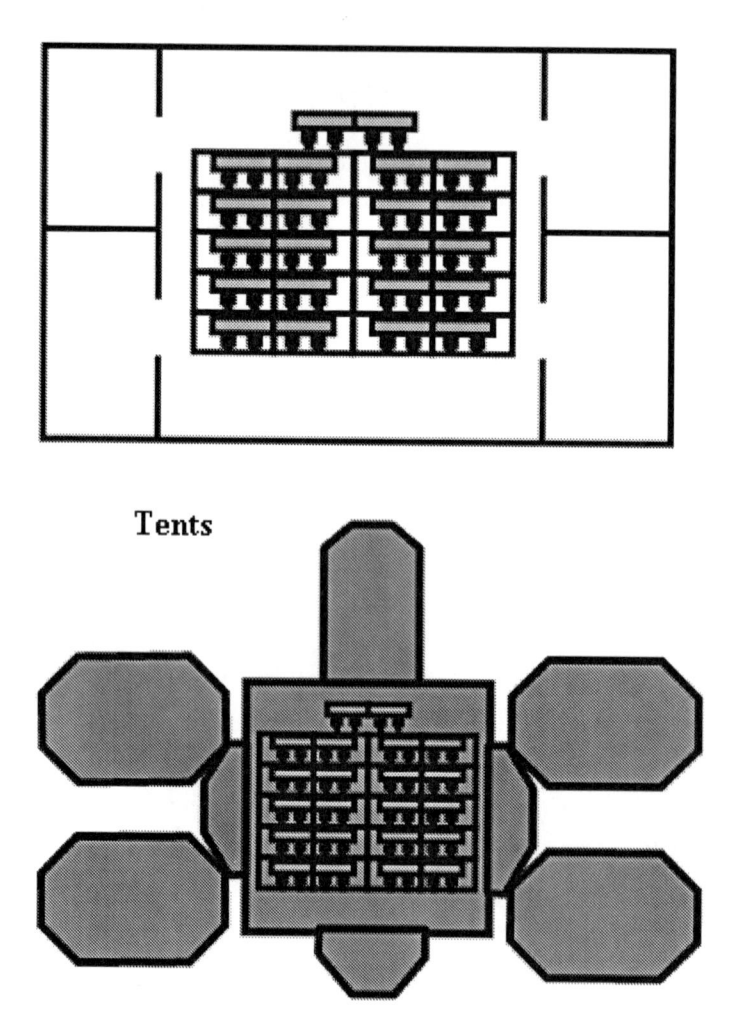

Tents

Figure 7, Example of building and/or tents

Logistics in Support of Disaster Relief

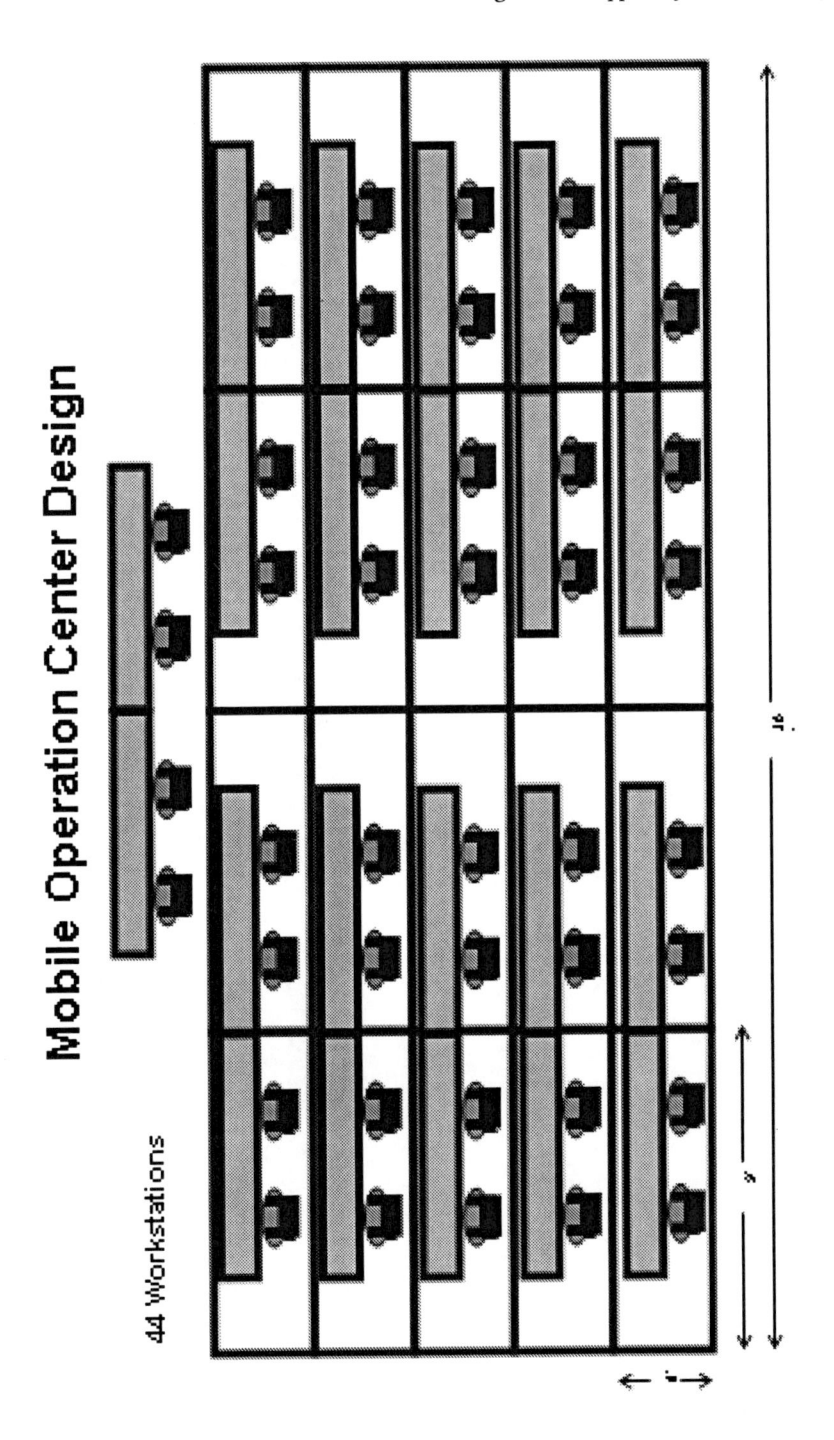

Figure 8, Example 1, of a Mobile Operations Center Design

James H. Henderson

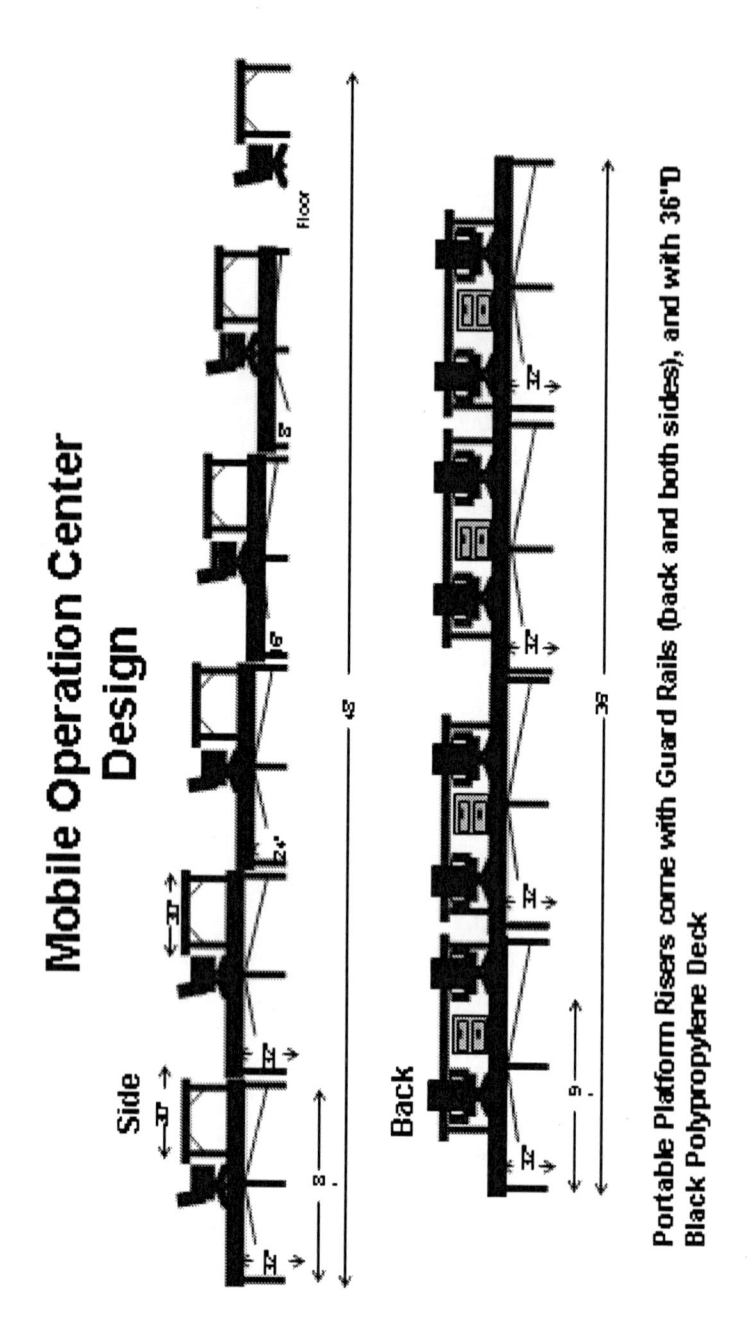

Figure 9, Example 2, of a Mobile Operations Center Design

CHAPTER 5

Disaster Relief Support Management

Concept

To provide the proper logistical support to a disaster area, I recommend to utilize a hybrid form of the military process called the Distribution Based Logistic System, as discussed in my previous book, "*The Process of Military Distribution Management; A Guide to Assist Military and Civilian Logisticians in Linking Commodities and Movement.*"

For easier reference, we will call this logistical support to a disaster area the Distribution Based Relief Support Process. The short answer is not to have redundancy of disaster relief supplies at both the federal and state levels, which would have to be stored, maintained and rotated for shelf life that would require a huge overhead of personnel and tax monies to manage and preserve in order to meet all situations. Bottom line is that the intermediate stocks forward at the state and county levels have a greater chance of being caught up in the disaster themselves and becoming destroyed wasting time and tax dollars. The key components to the whole process are **PLANNING, SYNCHRONIZATION, IMPLEMENTATION** and the integration of **IN-TRANSIT VISIBILITY**, between the federal and state agencies, to meet the supported areas consumption rates and time-definite delivery.

James H. Henderson

Structure and Control

The Federal Emergency Management Agency (FEMA) is funded to provide disaster relief support, as well as to maintain and manage relief supplies. This concept is sound because the intermediate stocks are not normally stored within the known disaster plane. In addition, we must understand that there are disasters other than hurricanes and earthquakes and that we cannot physically maintain stocks at all levels to support all scenarios. As you have probably gathered, I have not changed anything from the original concept. I have only added some new ideas, technology, processes, procedures, and guidelines to improve federal and state agencies corporation and management between the two. The bottom line here it is their responsibility to maintain and manage these stockpiles; they have been mandated and funded by Congress. What we must have in the system is the capability for visibility between federal and state agencies that can:

1. Gauge consumption rates of relief nodes forward.
2. Offer the capability to monitor the flow of these supplies forward.
3. Provide the visibility of disaster relief support commodities, as it moves on the highways forward, to facilitate a smooth transition of supplies from FEMA to State and Local agencies.

During Katrina, the real issue was that even with all the attempts of planning and synchronization there was no visibility of commodities moving forward, which provided a lack of time-definite delivery of commodities reaching the disaster areas. This problem makes it very difficult to predict when supplies could be transferred from federal to state agencies. The solution lies in adding the capability of In-Transit Visibility (ITV) giving a visual means to monitor and control the distribution network providing the capacity to validate or identify changes to the original plan so coordination and synchronization between the two levels of government can occur. By establishing this process early, federal agencies can move intermediate stocks of relief supplies forward and maintain this flow of commodities for an indefinite time frame. The system is built around management of inventory flows, rather than management of inventory levels in a disaster environment. The key ingredient in making this system work is In-Transit Visibility (ITV). By utilizing satellite communications technology it gives computer automation capability the relief support so that personnel can maintain the visibility of movement and commodities across the whole relief support distribution network.

Success here is measured by a degree of synchronization between the federal and state agencies to meet the supported areas consumption rates and time-definite delivery in a distribution infrastructure where forward logistic nodes are transit operations or Call Forward Areas (CFAs), rather than large Forward Distribution Point (FDP) supply stockpiles forward. Distribution Based Relief Support reduces the logistic footprint forward and extends operational reach and sustainability to expand the scope of support to a disaster area. Time-definite delivery is directly linked to both situational awareness and an agile Logistical Relief Support Process.

Disaster Relief Distribution Network

Under the Relief Support Process, the Forward Distribution Points would live off the flow, and there would be no need for intermediate stocks forward at the state level, which remember, requires housing, maintenance, and shelf life rotation that requires a huge overhead of personnel, monies to manage, and to maintain a disaster relief structure to meet all situations. The main concern is the distribution network that the logistician is required to operate within is as much an enemy as the disaster they are there to support. The limitations in the network's physical construction and our own resources can hamper our ability to conquer time, distance and space requirements in support of the relief areas. The concept needs the flexibility to adapt to the environment they are going to operate within, allowing the federal and state agencies to create hybrid versions or contingency plans, while providing operational procedures and structures to meet the needs of the distribution network and offer the proper disaster relief support setting. Logistical planners must have the vision to enhance the network with additional capabilities and tailor assets to meet shortfalls in reference to the physical infrastructure of the network and/or the resources required to support the flow of supplies. The Distribution Process in support of Disaster Relief is based on visibility of information, to maximize capacity of systems and to control the relief efforts forward. The goals of the federal and state agencies should be to create a force structure that is modular in composition and tailored by components to meet the situation or multiple situations as they occur. The U.S. Army has identified the importance in constructing a viable and sustainable distribution network in support of their own logistical operations, and has defined its key components in the doctrinal manual FM 3-0, Operation. In, Chapter 12-50, Combat Service Support Factors Influencing Operational Reach and Sustainability, it states;

> "The Army Combat Service Support (CSS) system in theater operates within the joint theater distribution system (see JP 4-01.4; FM 4-01.4). The distribution system consists of several interrelated networks: communications and automation, physical, and resource. These networks provide the asset visibility necessary for efficient and effective distribution. The communications and automation network distributes and correlates CSS data across the force, while assisting all commanders with management of the information. The physical network consists of the quantity and capability of fixed structures and established facilities. It includes factories, warehouses, airfields, seaports, roads, railroads, inland waterways, pipelines, terminals, bridges, tunnels, and buildings. These facilities can be located in CONUS, at an ISB, at a forward deployed base, or in theater. The resource network consists of the people, materiel, and machines operating within and over the physical network."[1]

With all this said, it is apparent that the distribution network is the logistician's operating space. Focusing on its construction, control and yes, even its manipulation, is a definite requirement for the success in supporting disaster relief efforts. Normally, disaster relief operations are conducted in a linear operational environment that can provide support to adjacent area of operations, which then can support an undeveloped distribution network. As the relief effort moves toward stability and sustainment operations, so does the distribution network progress to a nonlinear operational set, within either a contiguous or a noncontiguous

---

[1] FM 3-0 (formerly FM 100-5), *Operations*. 14 June 2001, 1-37.

area of operations. Nonlinear operations generally center on multiple critical points, which correlate to the logistical lines of communications (LOC) between operating bases within the distribution network. These lines of communications, or convoy routes that re-supply, are dependent on the ability to protect the element throughout its travel and predict its arrival time. However, when the freedom of movement in the lines of communications is threatened, linear operations should be considered. A problem exists when operating within a nonlinear operational set - every line of communication within the nonlinear construct, requires route clearing of disaster debris and could require convoy security, between specific boundaries and checkpoints leading to problem areas, as was seen in support of New Orleans during Operation Katrina. Operations like these add to the confusion and congestion of the relief distribution network, and take away relief and security forces to support convoy operations. To elevate the strain of these types of operations, federal, state and local agencies must synchronize subordinate unit actions in time, distance and space with the intent to link convoy operations with planned execution. To explain this synchronization, it is better the logistician establishes a battle rhythm between the daily distribution pushes and contingency stock levels based on the relief areas daily consumption rate and the delivery time, distance and space that are required to get supplies to meet Time Definite Delivery (TDD) requirements. Due to time, distance, and space, it may not be feasible to deliver all commodities each day. For example, the time and distance it takes one convoy to re-supply a Forward Distribution Point may take two days in duration to complete, thus making the logical re-supply cycle every three days. The space issue is different because the extent of the damaged area or other events can make that environment difficult to re-supply on a set cycle. For example - damages to the lines of communications, or events such as extreme weather can create circumstances that could temporarily halt re-supply of commodities to an area. This will then require additional commodities to be redistributed or retrograded from other supported regions, forward logistic nodes or to be diverted from federal strategic hubs, thus providing for continued re-supply until the time the standard re-supply cycle can resume. These are contingency stocks utilized during re-supply delays and surge operations. Daily consumption rates are forecasted and reported higher to adjust commodity re-supply rates to then compensate for missed rotation cycles to maintain the proper additional days of supply needed forward for contingency stocks, as well as required daily consumption stock. Remember, if the Forward Distribution Point lives off the flow and the flow equals the consumption rates, then any additional stocks forward can be designated for area support, contingency usage, or required rotation cycle of stocks. In support of this synchronization, the logistician produces a sustainment cycle, which is visible at all levels to provide situational awareness and synergy for planning and coordination between federal, state, and local staff elements. These scheduled re-supply operations are based on the beginning consumption rates and adjusted from reported data. Remember the support of past disaster relief efforts has made it apparent that in supporting relief operations, the logistician must push supplies forward with or without the requirement for a consistent reporting cycle. As long as the lines of communications are open and the original support cycle requirements known, then it is pushed regardless of any absence of reporting from the unit, or until the node or area does submit a report to adjust the cycle. Once the Initial Disaster Operations Stage is over, then an operational pause occurs and the disaster relief requirement moves to the Sustainment Disaster Operations Stage providing a more stable mode of support. A standard reporting and sustainment cycle is submitted and items are pushed by priority and importance to the node or area. For the concept to work, a distribution network has to be established from the beginning of relief operations to support an immature infrastructure, as well as to evolve over time to support the expectations of the projected mature infrastructure for future termination of relief support. Under this new distribution network structure, the federal and state agencies must establish and control the Main Supply Routes (MSR) and the local agencies, with the assistance from state authorities, establish and control Alternate Supply Routes (ASR). The combination of both types of routes as well as the incorporation of alternate modes of transportation (air, rail, and sea), the placement of in-transit visibility (ITV) devices throughout the network consisting of Radio Frequency Identification (RFID) tags, vehicle-tracking devices, fixed and hand-held interrogators capable, all provide the key components for tracking the flow of commodities and their movement. The planning and positioning of logistical support elements require integration to provide the proper configuration of the Disaster Relief Distribution Network. The following activities need proper placement within the network:

- Logistical Support Areas (LSA)
- Call Forward Areas (CFA)
- Forward Distribution Points (FDP)
- Rest Over Night Sites (RON)
- Movement Control Teams (MCT)
- Highway Regulation Teams (HRT)
- Security Checkpoints
- Distribution Management Teams (DMT)
- Other voluntary personnel for data collecting
- Tracking
- Reporting

The management of the Disaster Relief Distribution Network is imperative to logistical flow and the implementation of the Distribution Management Process. The Distribution Based Relief Support Process establishes a staff rhythm for movement control centered on a common operating picture between sustainment, movement and force protection, thus linking the three with in-transit visibility assets to improve force tracking and support distribution and ultimately providing synergy at all levels.

CHAPTER 6

Building the Relief Support Network

Perception

A key ingredient to making the overall process work is building the Relief Support Network. As stated before the plan is only as good as its implementation. The establishment of the Relief Support Network and its enablers requires systemic placement of communication, automation, personnel, and facilities to achieve the proper end state. Placement of the distribution enablers requires significant thought and coordination for the network to provide the proper in-transit visibility necessary to monitor the flow of commodities and equipment throughout the network (See Figure 10, Distribution Network Enablers).

Distribution Enablers
Road Network
Radio Frequency Identification (RFID) Tags
Interrogators
Movement Tracking Systems (Transponders)
Satellite Communications
Convoys
Command and Control System
Regional Staging Areas
Call Forward Areas
Distribution Point
Checkpoints

Figure 10, Distribution Network Enablers

Road Network

It seems too obvious, but you must already have the road network before the incident occurs. The requirement is to identify primary, secondary, and alternate road combinations that will be utilized in the event of a disaster for the purpose of evacuation or logistical support. The hardest part is recognizing all the different combinations of roads that could possibly be used to develop a network that will support the flow. The reason for this action is that you do not know which roads will be blocked due to damage and debris. Identifying the different road combination and laying out the inbound and outbound flow of traffic will enable you to develop a priority list of roads for clearing in the event one or more of the networks are blocked or damaged. Remember the establishment of the road network for support is a near-term requirement and must occur within the first 24-hours after a disaster. Look at Figure 11, Example of Road Network, avenues have been identified north and south, as well as east to west. These routes

Logistics in Support of Disaster Relief

can be coordinated with all essential organizations and agencies so all know the network where the rest of the enablers are placed.

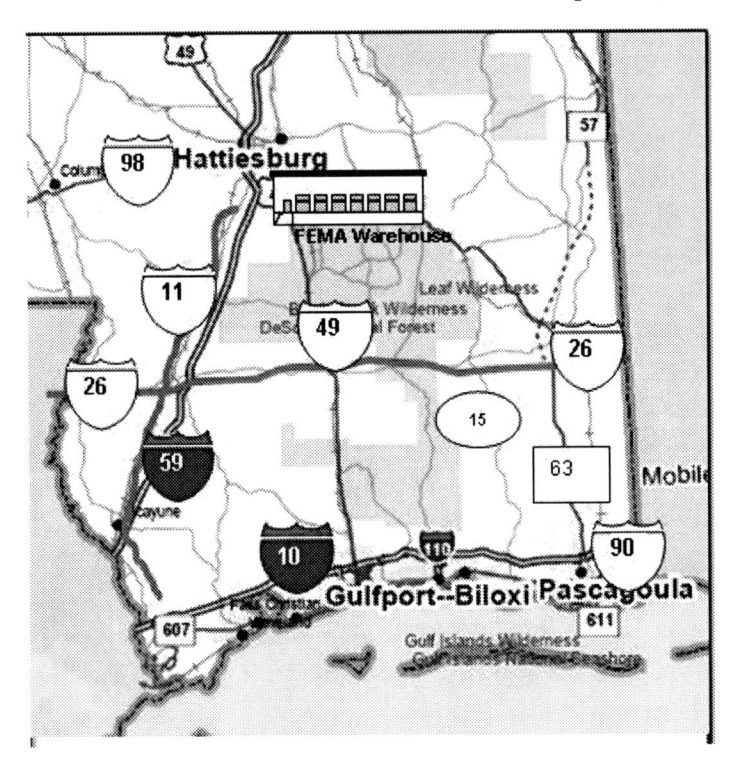

Figure 11, Example of Road Network

Radio Frequency Identification (RFID) System

The Radio Frequency Identification (RFID) system consists of transponder tags, antennas, Radio Frequency modules, readers and software. The devices are small electronic pieces of equipment that reflect and modify received continuous radio wave signals. The antennas broadcast and receive radio frequency signals generated by the Radio Frequency modules. The Radio Frequency modules also read and amplify returned signals prior to relaying them to a reader. The readers control the Radio Frequency modules. They receive the signals from the antenna and Radio Frequency module and transmit the data to a host computer or other logging device or system. The tags are not transmitters and do not radiate signals by themselves. They are either battery powered or have intermittent generator power, and will not send back an identification signal unless interrogated by a Reader. Battery powered tags will stay energized at all times. For the RFID model to work, each tag is attached to an object and programmed with identification information about that specific object. As the tagged object approaches an antenna, the antenna broadcasts a radio frequency signal towards it; the tag modifies the signal and transmits a signal that carries the identification code for the object back to the antenna. The antenna transmits the returning signal to the Radio Frequency module where it preconditions and amplifies it before sending it back to the reader. The reader interprets the Information Device (ID) code from the signal and validates the code based on user-defined criteria. It can also add useful information such as time and date to the code. The reader saves the ID codes in an internal storage buffer and transmits the codes to a host computer or other data-logging device. Once the RFID tag is identified by the integrators along the network, it sends the grid location where it was read and populates that information to the database thus creating a movement trail from start to finish. The database that is created displays on a web page showing a croniological listing of exactly when and where the RFID tag was detected (See Figure 12, How Radio Frequency Identification (RFID) System Work). There are two basic types of RIFD tags, active and passive. Active tags have an incorporated power supply or battery and passive tags have no power supply. Passive tags attain their power from the radio frequency provided by the reader through a method called inductive or capacitive coupling.

Logistics in Support of Disaster Relief

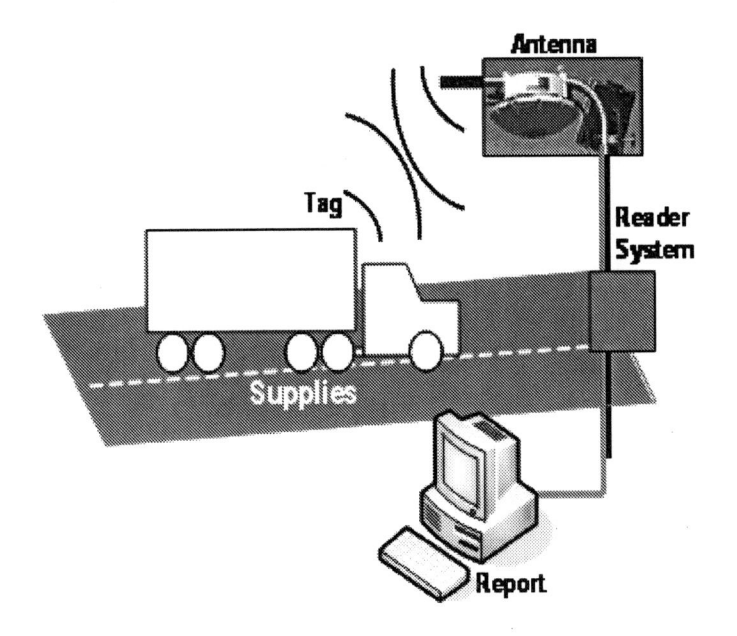

Figure 12, How Radio Frequency Identification (RFID) System Work

The following picture shows the way to tag a container with an Identification Bar Code Label and an RIFD tag for reading the tag itself by either a fix interrogator device or reading of the Bar Code Label with hand-held interrogators (See Figure 13). Labels and RIFD tags provide the capability for attachment to any type of shipment or commodity. The key to tagging a shipment is to place the label and RIFD tag in a safe and secure location on the item to protect from damage during movement. There is also new technology in labeling called smart labels consisting of an adhesive label with an RFID tag embedded inside. These tags can be encoded with changeable data and can be tested before printing the label. The label can contain all the bar codes, text and graphics used in earlier systems.

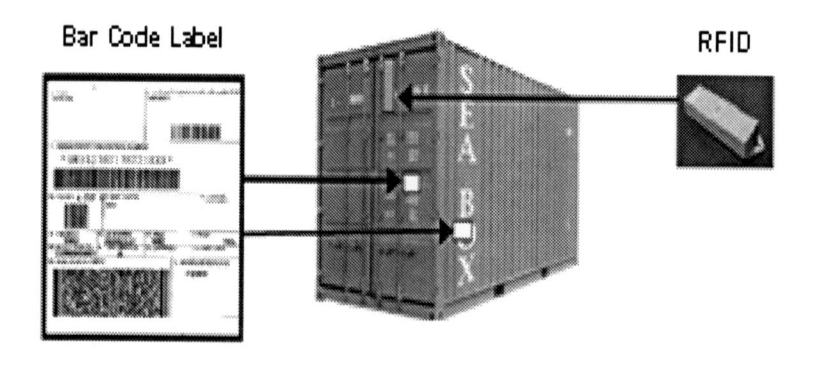

Figure 13, Example of container marked with an Identification Bar Code Label and RIFD tag

Interrogators

Interrogators are electronic devices that provide radio wave frequency interface between an antenna, the RFID tag, and a computer system. They generate radio frequencies, which in the case of passive tags powers the tag, through an antenna that sends and receives data from the RIFD tag. The device has a processor for managing the incoming data received from the tag, and then transmits information to the tag. The data received from the tag is encrypted and sent to the computer system for processing (See Figure 14).

Logistics in Support of Disaster Relief

Interrogator Network

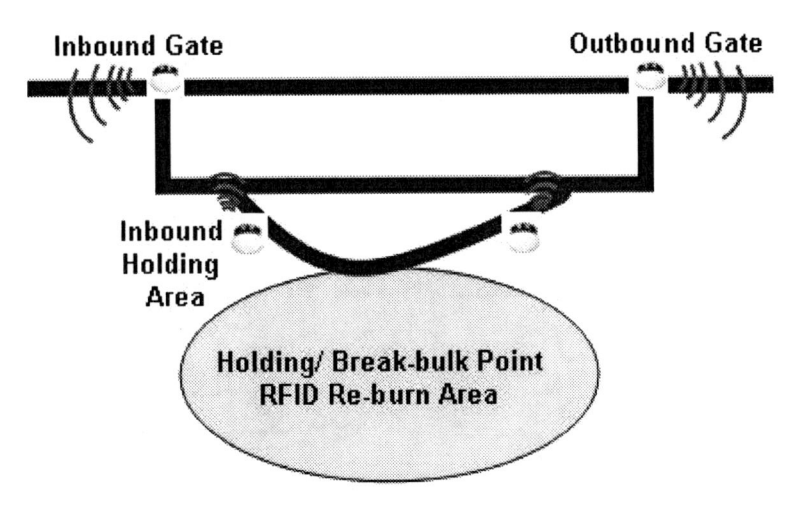

Inbound Gate　　　　　　　　**Outbound Gate**

Inbound Holding Area

Holding/ Break-bulk Point RFID Re-burn Area

Figure 14, How Interrogator System Works

The following pictures show examples fix interrogators used to identify RIFD tags, and hand-held interrogator devices used to read Bar Code (See Figure 15). There are a variety of fully integrated battery powered Hand-Held Interrogators and Readers which will enable the user to operate in extremely austere locations and capture desired data from any form of Automatic Identification Technology. The device provides the capability to identify, adjust, and/or correct the data as required at any given point in the Supply Chain. Some of the technology can provide a function to create a formatted message that enables easy transmission from other Automated Information Systems.

Fixed Interrogator

Hand-held Interrogator
Figure 15, Example of Fixed and Hand-held Interrogators

The following diagram, Figure 16, Example of Placing Fixed and Hand-held Interrogators, shows a possible example of placement of the interrogator technology along the road network.

Logistics in Support of Disaster Relief

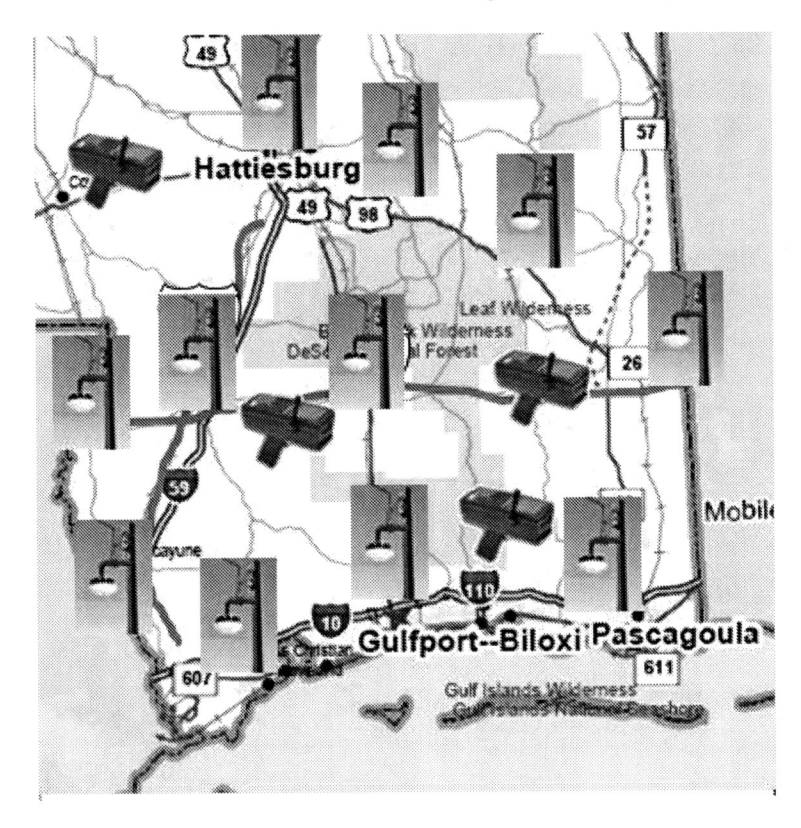

Figure 16, Example of Placing Fixed and Hand-held Interrogators

Satellite Devices for Movement Tracking Systems (Transponders)

Mobile Tracking Systems provide the capability for tracking vehicles and communicating during movement. These devices, called transponders, utilize a procedure consisting of mobile satellite two-way messaging that is wireless and flows from the tracking equipped vehicle to the control station. The mobile component (transponder) of the system is mounted on the vehicle and the control station component stays in communication within a prescribed timeframe to monitor vehicle locations giving near-real time tracking potential. This communication capability between the vehicle and control station requires a commercial satellite vendor that allows components to send and receive traffic. This type of technology allows the transportation coordinator to communicate with the operator of any vehicle, regardless of location (See Figure 17). New development integrates radio frequency technology and mobile tracking devices to provide the capability to read RIFD tags loaded on the vehicle using the vehicle mounted transponder to support in-transit visibility.

IN -TRANSIT VISIBILITY (ITV) SERVER

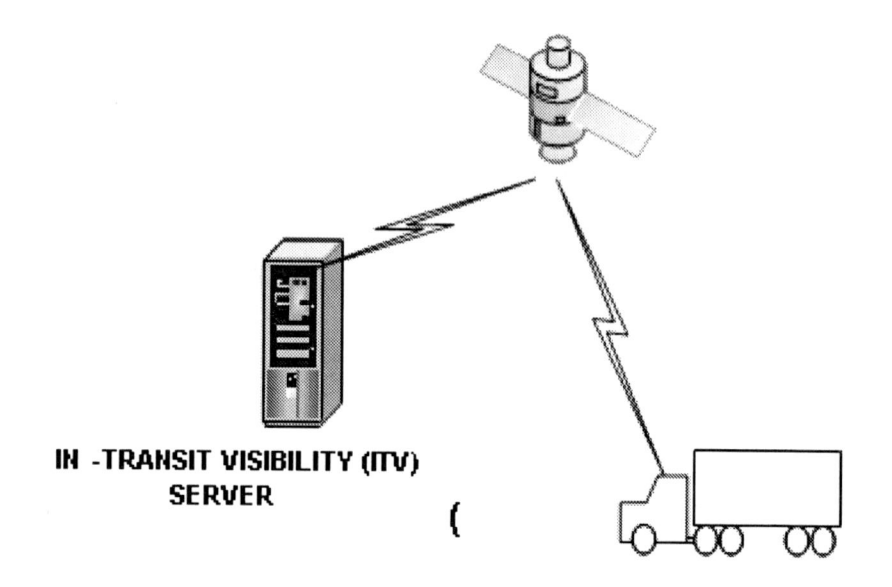

Figure 17, How Satellite Devices for Movement Tracking System Works

The following diagrams Figure 18, Examples of Satellite Tracking Devices, and Figure 19, Movement Tracking of multiple Transponders show an example of usage of mobile tracking technology, as well as different types of transponder devices utilized by the military and commercial vendors.

Logistics in Support of Disaster Relief

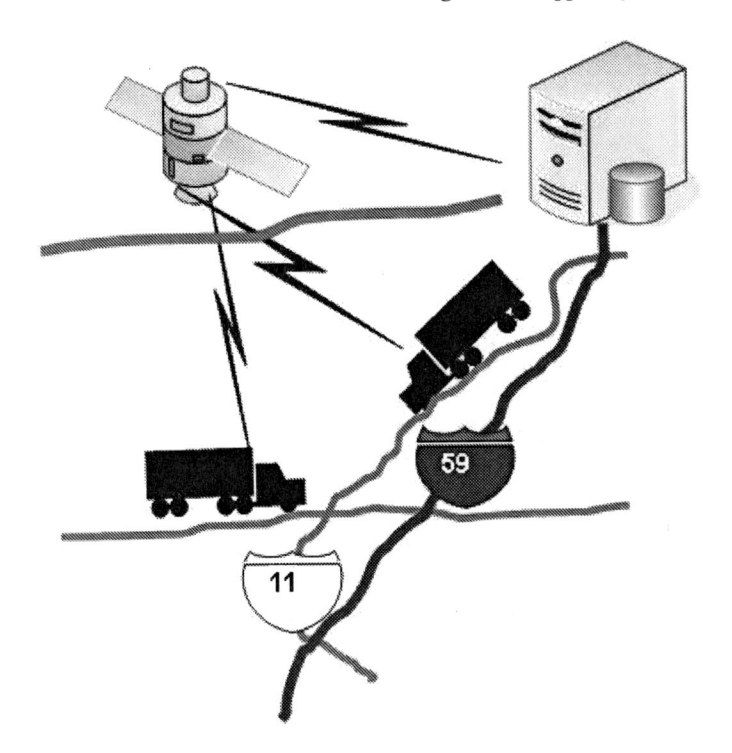

Figure 18, Example of Movement Tracking of multiple Transponders

Movement Tracking System (MTS)

James H. Henderson

VISTAR Satellite Tracking Device

Commercial Tracking Devices
Figure 19, Examples of Satellite Tracking Devices

Satellite Communication

A communications satellite is an artificial satellite stationed in space for the purpose of telecommunications. Satellite communication technology is used as a means to connect to the internet, television, cellular telephones, radio, and other forms of wireless communications. Connectivity consists of broadband data connections linking users who are located in very remote areas and cannot access a wire or cable connection.

Convoys

The best way to implement in-transit visibility for convoy tracking is to link the vehicles in any particular movement to a mobile tracking system or transponder, this process is called creating a virtual convoy. The convoy is scheduled on a movement table, which has all the data required to identify the number of vehicles and the manifests of commodity or equipment hauled. Once this is done the organization can track the lift or convoy as a virtual movement ,already having the schedule identifying the manifested items to be hauled, and the convoy and its vehicles being tracked with the mobile tracking transponder device. The contents of the convoy can have the manifests mounted to the mobile tracking device icon depicted on the graphical map of the computer system..,

Command and Control Systems

Another way to receive the information is using a command and control system, which displays the information from a graphical map depiction, providing a drill down capability to view the database listing. The U.S. Army and Marines use the Battle Command Sustainment Support System (BCS3), which is a common logistics command and control solution that provides an effective and efficient means to gather and integrate asset and in-transit information to manage the distribution and deployment missions. There is also a civilian version, the
Global Distribution Management System (GDMS), which provides a visual, map-centric, graphical tracking and data synthesis system that provides near real-time In-Transit Visibility (ITV) of moving and

deployable assets. These types of systems give the operator visibility of vehicle and commodity shipment movement across the network displayed on one computer.

Examples Network Enablers for Movement Tracking

An example of employment of Network Enablers for Movement Tracking (See Figure 20):
1. Virtual Convoy vehicle depicted on the automated information system stops movement.
2. Automated information system operator announces in the Operation Center;
"ATTENTION IN THE OPERATION CENTER, CONVOY #4, HAULING WATER, COTS, AND FOOD HAS ARRIVED AT DISTRIBUTION POINT #2, NORTH REGION, ARRIVING FROM ROUTE 206, 1200HRS, DEPARTURE TIME FOR RETURN TO CALL FORWARD AREA 1400HRS."
3. Operation Center notifies FEMA the return time of commercial vender vehicles, makes contact with State and Local officials within the zone of movement for them to make visual contact of the convoy and assist convoy in resuming its prescribed route of march.
4. Operation Center operator sends text message through the automated information system to the Mobile Tracking System assigned to the convoy, confirming closure of convoy and start time for next leg.
5. Automated information system operator can send text message through his terminal to the Mobile Tracking System base station.
6. If the Automated information system operator is unable to make contact with any of the Mobile Tracking Systems on his terminal, the operator can contact the nearest Checkpoint or Highway Route Team along the highway to stop the convoy and try to fix the problem.

Logistics in Support of Disaster Relief

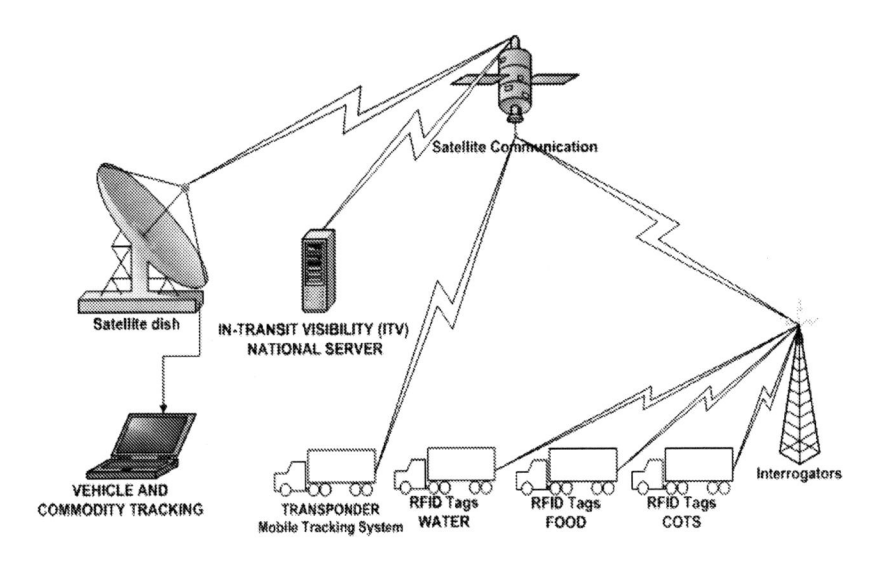

Figure 20, Employment of Network Enablers for Movement Tracking

Network Enablers for Route and Distribution Management

To round off the network enablers we need to discuss the physical aspect of the structure consisting of the actual support areas within the disaster area. These areas include Regional Staging Areas, Call Forward Areas, Distribution Points, and Checkpoints. Different echelons of government agencies operate and control these areas. For example, the Regional Staging Areas are mainly operated by federal agencies (FEMA), the Call Forward Areas are controlled by state agencies, the Distribution Points are primarily controlled and operated by local agencies, and Checkpoints can be a combination of both state and local agencies.

James H. Henderson

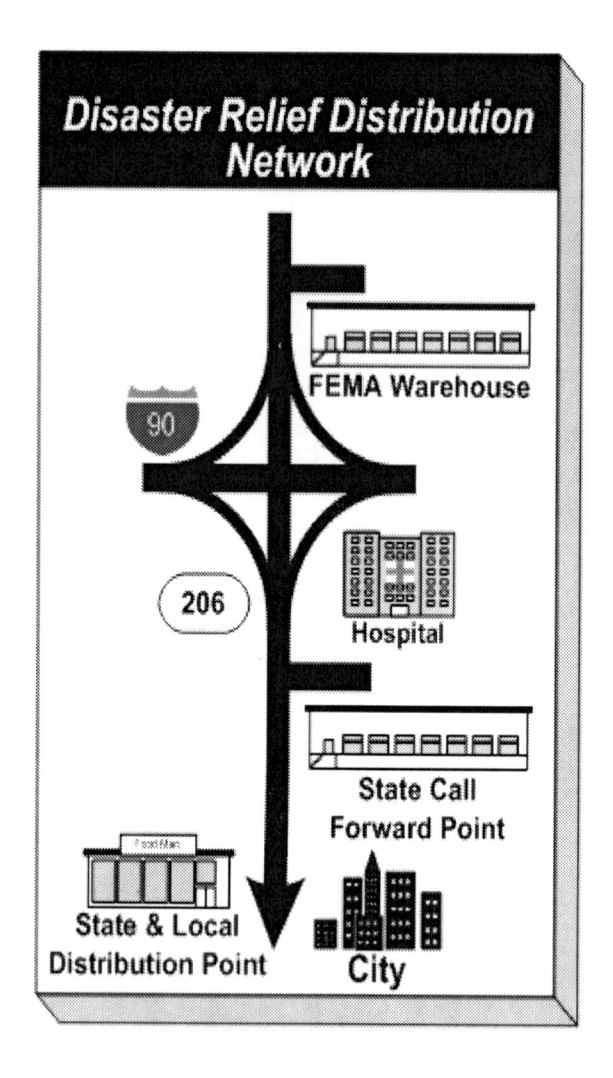

Figure 21, Network Enablers for Route and Distribution Management

Regional Staging Areas

These are the federal governments support areas usually operated by FEMA. This is where the federally requested equipment and supplies are shipped, received, and inventoried before being committed to the disaster area. This is also the location that supplies can be transferred to state control. Remember that all supplies at this location my not go forward, but could instead be there for contingency operations or if not required at this location be transferred to a different location or state for issue or storage. An example of such a facility is the mobile home trailer yard located in Purvis, Mississippi. There are literately acres of hundreds of mobile home trailers parked at this location for employment if required. The facility conducts trailer issue and turn-in, as well as transferring excess or required trailers to other areas or facilities. This facility is a good example of being close to the disaster plan, without putting the facility in immediate danger of destruction. The important muscle move that needs to happen at the Regional Staging Area is the hand-off of commodities and equipment as it is issued and moved forward to support the disaster area. This transfer of change of custody of supplies between the federal and state officials is important for commodity visibility forward as it moves across the disaster support network. This is the first time in-transit visibility begins within the disaster network and a smooth hand-off of identification device information is required so the state and local agencies can continue to track the supplies to their final destination. As these supplies, move forward state and local officials need to track this flow against requirements and project their arrival so support cycle reporting can be gauged and tracked to identify old and completed requests and to establish new requirements.

Call Forward Areas

Call Forward Areas can have a combination of federal and state employees, but are primarily operated by state officials. This is the location the state and local authorities receive and hold commodities and equipment until directed to move forward in support of one of the Distribution Points. As higher provides the requirements and timeframe for movement of supplies forward, the area officials create convoys and begin the pushing of supplies and equipment to the required Distribution Points. This location has life support and maintenance requirements for the workers and the vehicles to operate the facility. Some of the logistical requirement is not only for the facility itself, an example is fuel for the vehicles and refrigerated refers being used to haul the commodities forward. This location has to be thought through and planned accordingly prior to its establishment. Insure the plan reflects the proper land space and support requirements needed to create a working transfer point over an unpredicted time. Once the requirement is identified to send commodities forward, the in-transit visibility process continues within the disaster network so the state and local agencies can continue to track the supplies to their final destination. As these supplies move forward they are tracked against requirements, their arrival time is projected so support cycle reporting are gauged and tracked to identify completed requests and institute new requirements.

Distribution Points

The Distribution Points forward are the final spot for the in-transit visibility process, but the beginning of the reporting process to identify to higher the commodities and supplies required to support the location. So really, the Distribution Point begins and ends the in-transit visibility process by identifying the supplies required and visually tracking the commodities to there final destination. The Distribution Points locations are operated by state, local and volunteer organizations and agencies, and are where the real interaction with the population affected occurs. These points can distribute supplies, provide shelter, feeding, medical treatment, etc., and will require life support and maintenance not only for the employees operating the facility, but also for disaster victims. These locations need to be planned and several different sites projected which will best support the disaster requirement.

Checkpoints

Checkpoints are required to assist in the management of traffic flow and control choke points within the road network for movement in and out of the disaster area. These checkpoints are man intensive, but with the proper enablers (communication and automation) coordinated and established early in the operations these requirements can be multi-tasked to facilitate command and control along the road network. This will provide visibility of operations and monitor commodity flow. Portable or fixed interrogators can be placed at these points for over-watch of system operation and maintenance. The majority of the time checkpoints are established at key intersections or chokepoints that can

Logistics in Support of Disaster Relief

provide important information on traffic flow or in-transit visibility of commodities. Local authorities and police are going to establish checkpoints to control access to the disaster area, so you should use them as well for dual purposes when possible.

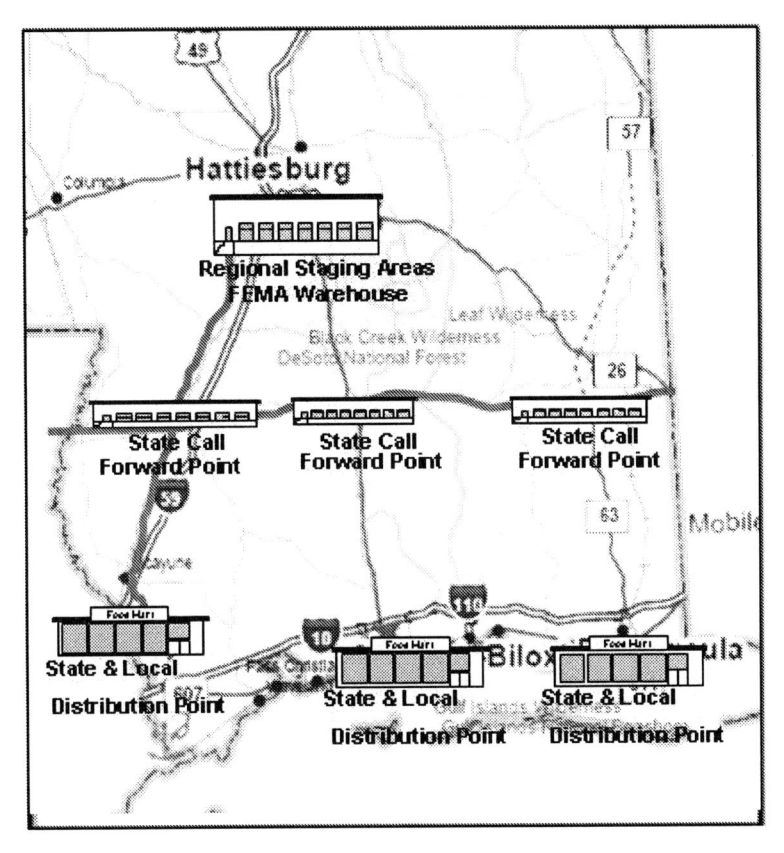

Figure 22, Example of a Disaster Relief Support Physical Structure Lay Out

CHAPTER 7
Relief Support Process

Process

Relief Support Process synchronizes critical supply and transportation assets to facilitate disaster sustainment tracking, and to provide a visual graphical picture of distribution flow in support of the four stages of disaster relief support. The process encompasses a 72 through 24 N-hours, continuing on into the operations with an initial stage of 1 through 96 N+hours, leading into the sustainment stage consisting of a 120 through End State hours, and ultimately closing with a one week after operations completion N+hour sequence. The stages based around the four key components of the process, consisting of *Planning*, *Synchronization*, *Implementation*, and the integration of *In-Transit Visibility*.

Operations

Just like any well-structured plan, the operation is broken up into stages to support command and control, providing staff elements a way to identify completion of critical objectives and the starting point of new initiatives. The stages are designed to encompass the complete operation from pre-disaster, continuing through the sustainment portion, and ultimately to closure. The time frame consists of the following phases:

- **Stage I: Pre-Disaster Operations (N-72 – N-48 hours):** Begins by establishing ground rules between the different levels of government and civilian agencies by conducting planning meeting to construct and coordinate a workable disaster relief support plan. This is done by regions consisting of projections and alert procedures to identify and notify available assets (personnel, equipment, and supplies) in support of the disaster area.

- **Stage II: Initial Disaster Operations (N-24 – N+96 hours):** This stage starts with the coordination and implementation of required supplies and the hand-off of these commodities from federal, thru state, and ultimately to local agencies for distribution. It is also necessary to direct and manage the placement and establishment of the Distribution Enablers, which builds the Disaster Relief Distribution Network based on the initial plan. The final function is the establishment of information systems to assist the staff levels in supply flow management.
- **Stage III: Sustainment of Disaster Operations (N+120 – N+ End State hours):** In this stage, the operations begin to stabilize allowing the staff and relief personnel to develop a staff rhythm. This continuity allows the workforce to predict and eventually get ahead of the relief support required, ultimately moving the supported communities that much closer to recovery. If the capability of in-transit visibility has been established properly, the staff will begin to manage supply flow and initiate the redistribution of commodities across supported regions and distribution points. The last step is to initiate the development of a Closure Plan between the different levels of government and civilian agencies.
- **Stage IV: Closure of Disaster Operations (N+ End State hours – N+ Closure-one week after completion):** The last stage centers on the Management of Supply Flow and the Retrograde of commodities and personnel forward, as well as the execution of the Closure Plan. Once the operation is complete, officials conduct an After Action Review (AAR), publish lessons learned, and update the Disaster Relief Support Plans.

Objective

For the above stages of disaster support operations to be completed, an important objective must be accomplishing during Stage III: Sustainment of Disaster Operations (N+120 – N+ End State hours). The military personnel (Active Duty, Reserve, or National Guard Units) conducting support operations will break contact as quickly as possible. This requires conclusion of the support mission to the point that local government and non-government agencies can assume control and continue stability and sustainment operations. As in any coordinated and orchestrated plan, a main objective must be accomplished before the operation can begin to move to closure. This objective is that the support Lines of Communication (LOC) will move from a linear to a non-linear movement table, thus providing for redistribution of supplies from other Forward Distribution Points (FDP) to relocate laterally across the disaster area of operation. The key goals required to accomplish this objective are:

1. Routes cleared of debris laterally connecting the linear supply routes coming from the Call Forward Area (CFA).
2. Connect these routes creating a circular movement table from the Call Forward Area and the Forward Distribution Points across the entire disaster area.
3. Conduct redistribution of commodities laterally to different Forward Distribution Points across the disaster area.

To clarify this idea during Stage II: Initial Disaster Operations (N-24 – N+96 hours) and the beginning of Stage III: Sustainment of Disaster Operations (N+120 – N+ End State hours) the Lines of Communications leaving the Call Forward Area in support of the Forward Distribution Points are established generally in a linear construct. This is mainly due to the makeup of the disaster environment after the event has left debris and physical devastation literally across the disaster area. In this situation of routes, to redistribute commodities from one Forward Distribution Point to another across the disaster area of operations the operators would have to convoy down to the Forward Distribution Point having the commodity and load the item. Then convoy back to the Call Forward Area in support of the disaster area, and then convoy on a different route to the Forward Distribution Point requiring the commodities or items. This is too time consuming; it is almost easier and faster to load the convoy with the required commodities or items from the Call Forward Area and convoy to the Forward Distribution Point needing the supplies. The problem with this is it creates excess supplies forward that then have to be retrograded later, as well as require additional supplies to be used to support the operation when there are ones that are already located forward in the disaster area, but are in the wrong location to support the mission. All this creates redundancy of commodities and additional expenditures of funding in support of the disaster operations (See Figure 23, Linear Supply Routes from the Call Forward Area to the Forward Distribution Points).

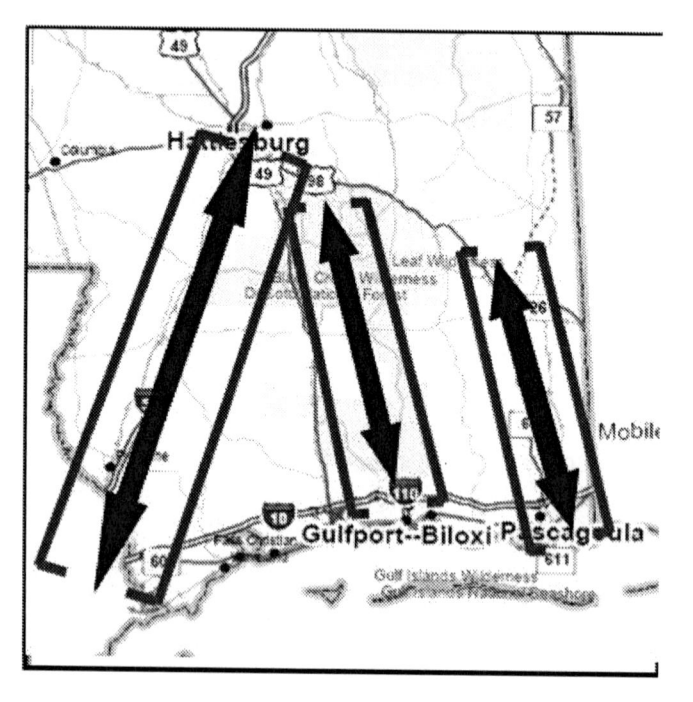

Figure 23, Linear Supply Routes from the Call Forward Area to the Forward Distribution Points

The ultimate goal is achieved at some point during Stage III: Sustainment of Disaster Operations (N+120 – N+ End State hours) when the Lines of Communications leaving the Call Forward Area in support of the Forward Distribution Points are reestablished in a nonlinear construction. By creating a lateral route across the disaster area of operations, you have linked the Forward Distribution Points,

Logistics in Support of Disaster Relief

and established a circular movement table from the Call Forward Area to the different Forward Distribution Points and back to the original Call Forward Area of origin. This enables the convoys leaving the Call Forward Area to travel carrying supplies to the first Forward Distribution Point and drop off items and reload other items required at different points located within the disaster area. The convoy leaves the first Forward Distribution Point and travels to all the nodes located on the route redistributing items and ultimately returning to the original Call Forward Area. By creating this new movement table, we can redistribute commodities across the disaster area without having to make excess convoys, provide a more timely support cycle, and begin to assist retrograde operations which is a key goal for Stage IV: Closure of Disaster Operations (N+ End State hours – N+ Closure-one week after completion). (See Figure 24, Nonlinear Supply Routes from the Call Forward Area to the different Forward Distribution Points and back).

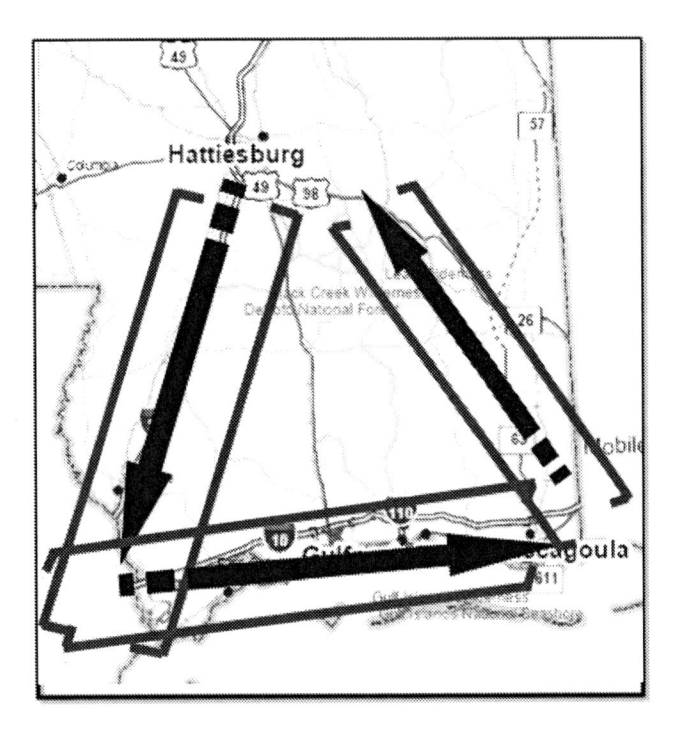

Figure 24, Nonlinear Supply Routes from the Call Forward Area to the different Forward Distribution Points and back.

By identifying the process for the operation, and establishing the missions required, it becomes evident that there are objectives, with key goals, that need completion before an organization can declare success. This book is a planning guide to assist civilian and military leaders, and if military personnel are utilized it is imperative that the military disengage as soon as possible and hand-off the execution of support operations to local government and non-governmental agencies. Therefore the key objective, in moving a disaster relief support effort that much closer to end state and closure, could be as easy as accomplishing the above objective of redistribution of commodities in a circular movement which links all the Forward Distribution Points laterally across the entire disaster area of operations.

CHAPTER 8

Pre-Disaster Operations

Stage I: Pre-Disaster Operations

Pre-Disaster Operations (N-72 – N-48 hours) is probably the most important stage of the whole process in that it begins by establishing ground rules between the different levels of government and civilian agencies. If government officials have gathered all the responsible and influential personnel to conduct planning and coordination meetings, this will construct a workable and executable disaster relief support plan. This plan should be constructed by regions consisting of projections and alert procedures to identify and notify available assets (personnel, equipment, and supplies) in support of the disaster area.

The stage should also consist of a series of tests and exercises, which will certify and adds validity to the plan. These tests and exercises are to be conducted agency pure at first, but eventually should migrate into interagency collective exercises to stress the synchronization and implementation of the plan. The important points evaluated during the tests and exercises consist of the management of resources and information. Also, to stress the importance of interaction between levels of command, and how in-transit visibility of assets and commodities can provide synergy among the different staff levels ultimately providing the critical information required for the stages of disaster relief operations to progress. The complete Stage I – Pre Disaster Operations (N-72 – N-48 hours) can be visualized in its entirety below in Figure 25.

James H. Henderson

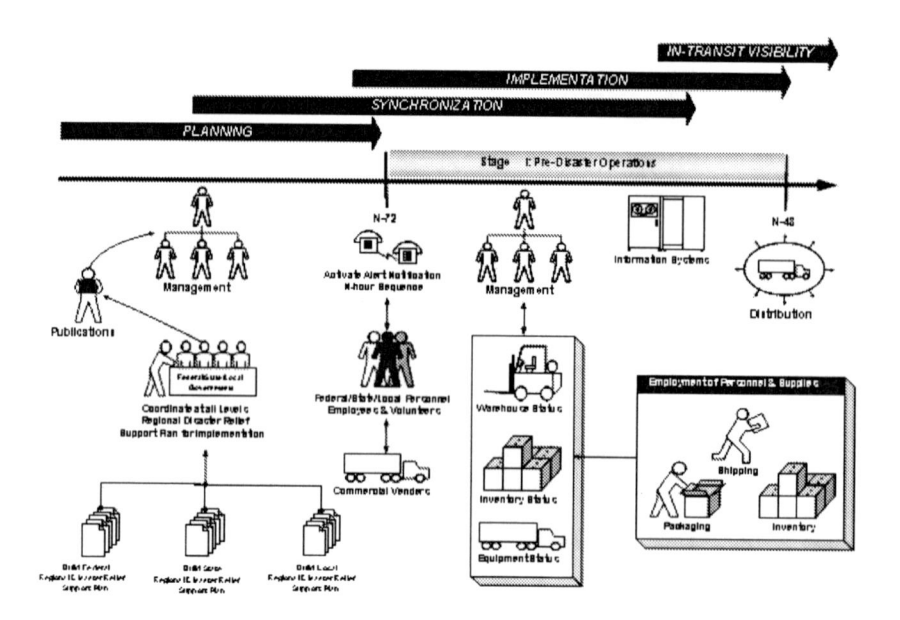

**Figure 25, Stage I: Pre-Disaster Operations
(N-72 – N-48 hours)**

Planning

Government and civilian agencies at all levels must conduct planning and coordination meetings to identify all supplies and necessities required to support the disaster victims, as well as those required to support and maintain sustainment of the operation over a long period of time. Commodities, equipment, personnel, etc. all have to be taken into consideration when developing a good logistical support plan. Once the plan is constructed, it must be tested to validate that it is a workable and executable disaster relief support plan. Testing can be conducted inter-agency or collectively across all levels of staff elements. Understand this is the hardest part, but without this exercising of the plan you will not identify shortfalls due to more coordination between agencies, or lack of individual training needed to implement the plan/operations. The following Stage I – Planning Objective Checklist and Diagram Insert (See Figure 26) is provided for review:

Logistics in Support of Disaster Relief

- Stage I– Planning Objective Checklist
    1. Develop a Regional Disaster Relief Support Plan
    2. Coordinate at all Levels Regional Disaster Relief Support Plan for Implementation
    3. Produce and distribute publications of the approved Disaster Relief Support Plan to all levels of government and civilian agencies.
    4. Implement Management and Training of plan.
    5. Conduct interagency collective exercises to stress the synchronization and implementation of the plan.

Stage I– Planning Diagram Insert, Figure 26

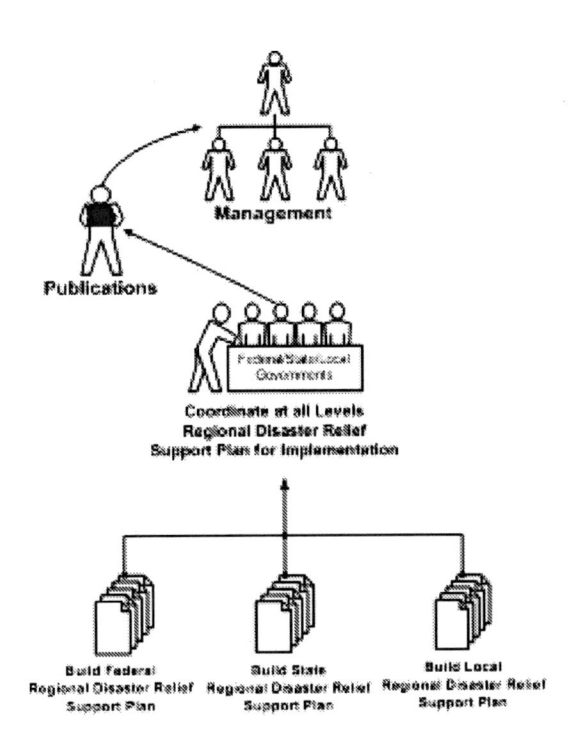

Synchronization

Initiate alert procedures to notify available assets (personnel, equipment, and supplies) in support of the disaster area. Also begin identifying known volunteer organizations, groups, or individual that are available to assist in the relief support effort. This is an ongoing list, some maybe ready to work immediately, others are available once they themselves have regrouped from the disaster effects, and some even later in the effort due to news coverage and their willingness to assist the victims. This is a vast pool of personnel that if organized and utilized in the right manner can make a great difference in the number and time length of shift work at the different support locations within the disaster regions. The following Stage I – Synchronization Objective Checklist and Diagram Insert (See Figure 27) is provided for review:

- *Stage I– Synchronization Objective Checklist*
    1. Activate Alert Notification N-hour Sequence
    2. Federal/State/Local Personnel Employees & Volunteers
    3. Commercial Venders

Stage I– Synchronization Diagram Insert, Figure 27

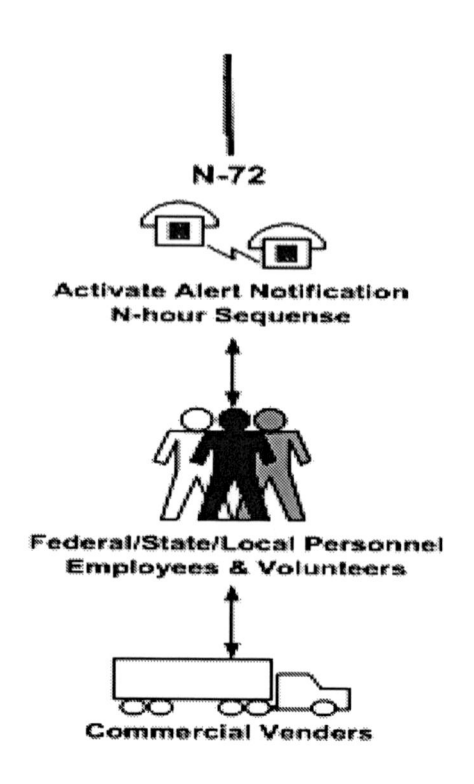

Logistics in Support of Disaster Relief

Implementation

This is the management of supply flow and its capability of maintaining initial requirements across the supported area of operations (AOR). The following Stage I – Implementation Objective Checklist and Diagram Insert (See Figure 28) is provided for review:

- *Stage I– Implementation Objective Checklist*
  1. Management Supply Flow.
  2. Coordinate requirements across supported Regions and Distribution Points.
  3. Manage Warehouse, Inventory, and Equipment Status.
  4. Employment of Personnel and Supplies (Inventory-Packing-Shipping)

Stage I– Implementation Diagram Insert, Figure 28

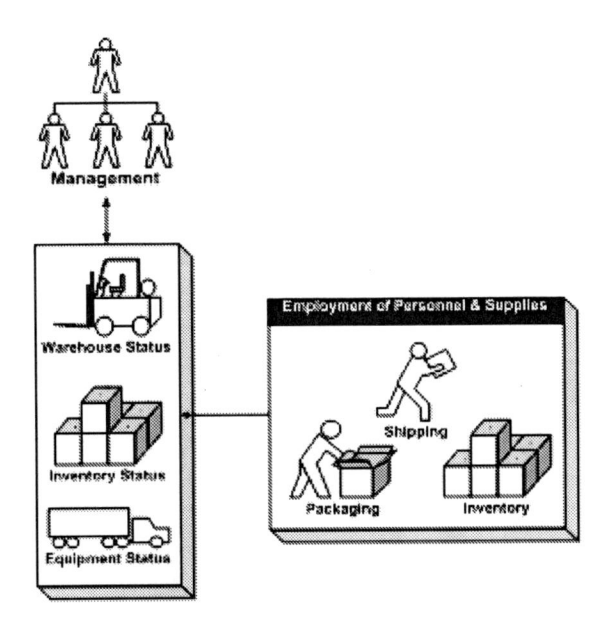

In-Transit Visibility

Utilizing automated Command and Control Information Systems staffs can have situational awareness of the Disaster Relief Distribution

Network to; (1) anticipate logistical needs (2) integrate supply and services (3) synchronize logistical support to facilitate priorities and (4) optimize assets for present and future operational support. In-Transit Visibility provides staff sections visibility of movement, the capacity of supply nodes, and the control over the network. The basic technology is for Transponders or Interrogators to send data to a satellite that then sends it to a system of record server, which feeds command and control information systems. Example of a command and control information system the U.S. Army utilizes is Battle Command Sustainment Support System (BCS3). It is really quite simple, because this is how the logistical operation works at Regional Distribution Centers or Distribution Terminals sustainment provider begin loading platforms, identifies In-Transit Visibility (ITV) devices (transponders), building manifests and linking Radio Frequency Identification Devices (RFID) with convoys. Convoy's moves down the network and transponder on a set time, send a signal of location, mounted manifest information to the satellite, and thus update the server and information system. In addition, as convoy pass fix or hand-held interrogators, RFID tags are read and based on a prescribed timeframe the interrogator sends to satellite and thus updates the server and information system. The following Stage I – In-Transit Visibility Objective Checklist and Diagram Insert (See Figure 29) is provided for review:

- *Stage I– In-Transit Visibility Objective Checklist*
1. Provide Command and Control of the Disaster Relief Distribution Network by the Management of Information Systems to give visibility of assets and commodities as they move across the network. The basic technology is for Transponders or Interrogators send data to a satellite that sends to the system of record server, which then feeds the information systems. Example of a command and control information system the U.S. Army utilizes is Battle Command Sustainment Support System (BCS3).
2. Conduct distribution tracking of convoys and commodities as it moves across the Disaster Relief Distribution Network. Example of types of hardware that could be utilized consist of the following:

a. Convoys
- Satellite Communications – Capability to receive data from mobile transponders and send to information system for tracking.
- Transponders
  - MTS – Movement Tracking System
  - DTRACS – Defense Tracking System
  - DynaFleet – Volvo Commercial System
  - PanaTracker – Commercial System
  - VISTAR – Commercial System
  - Cell Phone Tracking Capability

b. Commodities
- Satellite Communications – Capability to receive data from fixed or hand-held interrogators and send to information system for tracking.
- RFID - Radio Frequency Identification Devices
  - Transponders Tags (Sustainment and Vehicle)
  - Antennas
  - Radio Frequency Modules
  - Readers
  - Software
- Bar Code Labels
- Fixed Interrogator
- Hand-held Interrogators
- Early Entry Deployment Support Kit (EEDSK)

Stage I – In-Transit Visibility Diagram Insert, Figure 29

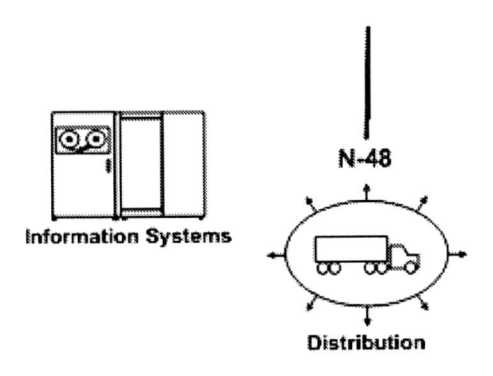

CHAPTER 9

Initial Disaster Operations

Stage II: Initial Disaster Operations

The Initial Disaster Operations (N-24 – N+96 hours) stage starts with the coordination and implementation of required supplies and the hand-off of these commodities from federal to state, and ultimately to local agencies for distribution. It is also necessary to direct and manage the placement and establishment of the Distribution Enablers, which builds the Disaster Relief Distribution Network based on the initial plan. Remember, the initial plan may not be executable after the disaster has concluded its damage of the surrounding environment, so additional coordination may be required before operations may begin. The final function is the establishment of information systems to assist the staff levels in supply flow management. If the capability of in-transit visibility is implemented correctly, the pertinent information will be provided to achieve a successful result.

The Initial Disaster Stage consists of the implementation of the scheduled re-supply operations based on beginning consumption rates, which will then be adjusted as the stage matures, and reliable reporting data is obtained. As long as the lines of communications are open and whatever the beginning support cycle is at that time, the required amount is pushed regardless of an absence any reporting from the unit, or until the node or area does submit a report to adjust the cycle. The complete Stage II: Initial Disaster Operations (N-24 – N+96 hours)is visible in its entirety below in Figure 30.

James H. Henderson

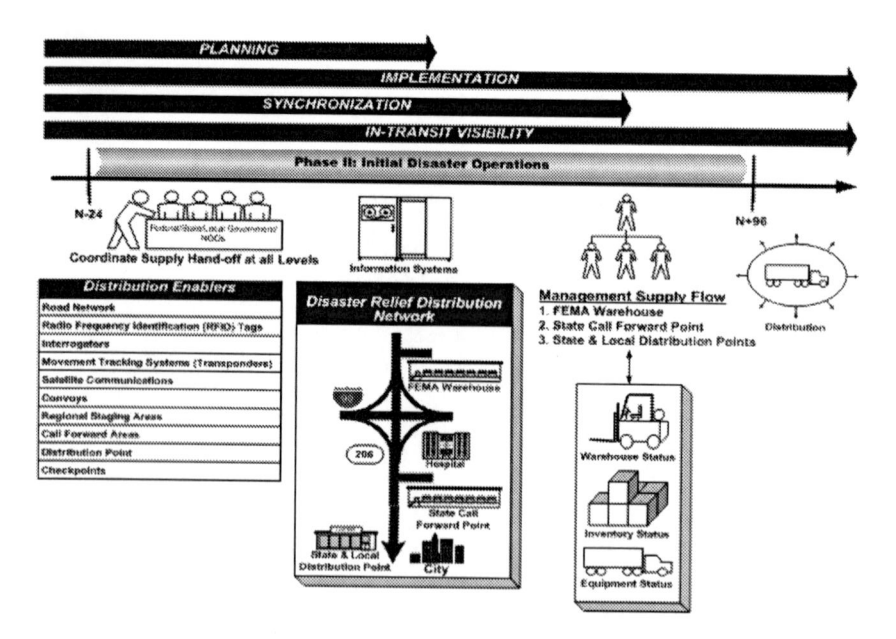

Figure 30, Stage II: Initial Disaster Operations (N-24 – N+96 hours)

Planning

This is the staff's opportunity to begin the execution of the plan and conduct coordination of the plan itself. It is also the time for the staff to test and verify the proper placement of the distribution enablers. The following Stage II – Planning Objective Checklist and Diagram Insert (See Figure 31)is provided for review:

- *Stage II – Planning Objective Checklist*
  1. Coordinate Supply Hand-off at all Levels
  2. Coordinate Distribution Enablers

Stage II – Planning Diagram Insert, Figure 31

N-24

Federal/State/Local Government/ NGOs

Coordinate Supply Hand-off at all Levels

Distribution Enablers
Road Network
Radio Frequency Identification (RFID) Tags
Interrogators
Movement Tracking Systems (Transponders)
Satellite Communications
Convoys
Regional Staging Areas
Call Forward Areas
Distribution Point
Checkpoints

Synchronization

This is the time to bring together all of the automation, communication, physical, and resource enablers to enhance the visibility over the disaster relief distribution network. The following Stage II – Synchronization Objective Checklist and Diagram Insert (See Figure 32) is provided for review:

- *Stage II – Synchronization Objective Checklist*
  1. Establish communications channels to support Information Systems that will facilitate situational awareness.

2. Establish a complete Disaster Relief Distribution Network providing an infrastructure that supports conditions.

Stage II – Synchronization Diagram Insert, Figure 32

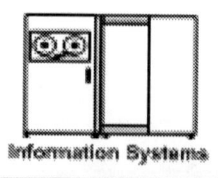

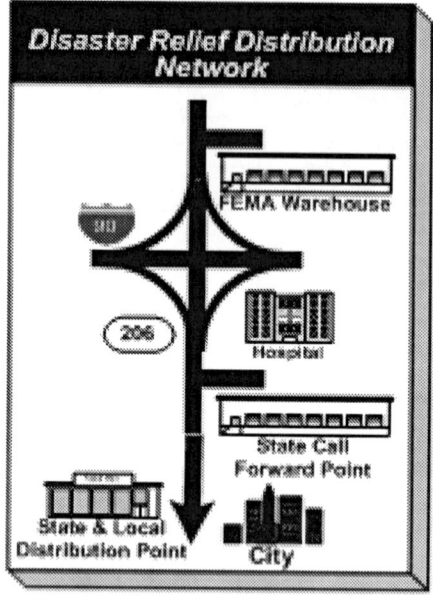

Implementation

The execution of managing supply flow and the ability to capture the forecasting and reporting requirements needed to support forward demands. The following Stage II –Implementation Objective Checklist and Diagram Insert (See Figure 33)is provided for review:

- *Stage II – Implementation Objective Checklist*
  1. Management of Supply Flow.
  2. Coordinate Reporting Flow of required and forecasted commodities across supported Regions and Distribution Points.

3. Manage Warehouse, Inventory, and Equipment Status.

Stage II – Implementation Diagram Insert Figure 33

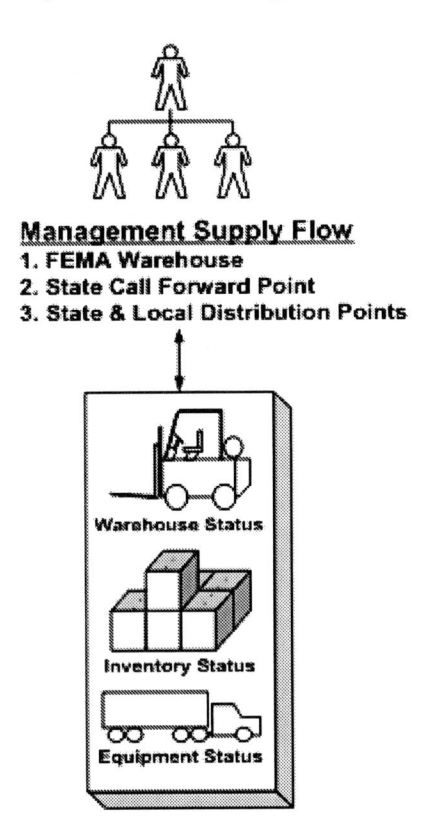

Management Supply Flow
1. FEMA Warehouse
2. State Call Forward Point
3. State & Local Distribution Points

Warehouse Status
Inventory Status
Equipment Status

In-Transit Visibility

This information is the same for all four stages, it bears repeating, as it is an essential element of every stage. Utilizing automated Command and Control Information Systems a staff can have situational awareness of the Disaster Relief Distribution Network to; (1) anticipate logistical needs (2) integrate supply and services (3) synchronize logistical support to facilitate priorities and (4) optimize assets for present and future operational support. In-Transit Visibility provides staff sections visibility of movement, the capacity of supply nodes, and the control over the network. The basis for this technology is for Transponders or Interrogators to send data to a satellite that sends to a system of record server, which feeds a command and control information systems. Remember the example of a command and control information system the U.S. Army utilizes is Battle Command Sustainment Support System (BCS3). It is really very simple because this is how the logistical operation works a Regional Distribution Center or Distribution Terminals sustainment provider begins loading platforms, identifies In-Transit Visibility (ITV) devices (transponders), building manifests and links Radio Frequency Identification Devices (RFID) with convoys. Convoy moves down the network and transponder on a set time, send signal of location, mounted manifest information to satellites, and thus update the server and information system. Also, remember that as a convoy passes fix or hand-held interrogators RFID tags read and based on a prescribed timeframe the interrogator sends to the satellite and thus it updates the server and information system. The following Stage II – In-Transit Visibility Objective Checklist and Diagram Insert (See Figure 34) provided for review:

- *Stage II – In-Transit Visibility Objective Checklist*
    1. Provide Command and Control of the Disaster Relief Distribution Network by use of the Management of Information Systems to give visibility of assets and commodities as they move across the network. Notethe importance of the Transponders or Interrogators send data to the satellite that then will send it to system of record server and then feeds to the information systems.
    2. Conduct distribution tracking of convoys and commodities as it moves across the Disaster Relief Distribution Network. Example of types of hardware that could be utilized consist of the following:
        a. Convoys
            - Satellite Communications – Capability to receive data from mobile transponders and send to information system for tracking.
            - Transponders
                - MTS – Movement Tracking System
                - DTRACS – Defense Tracking System
                - DynaFleet – Volvo Commercial System

Logistics in Support of Disaster Relief

- PanaTracker – Commercial System
- VISTAR – Commercial System
- Cell Phone Tracking Capability

b. Commodities
- Satellite Communications – Capability to receive data from fixed or hand-held interrogators and send to information system for tracking.
- RFID - Radio Frequency Identification Devices
  - Transponders Tags (Sustainment and Vehicle)
  - Antennas
  - Radio Frequency Modules
  - Readers
  - Software
- Bar Code Labels
- Fixed Interrogator
- Hand-held Interrogators
- Early Entry Deployment Support Kit (EEDSK)

Stage II– In-Transit Visibility Diagram Insert, Figure 34

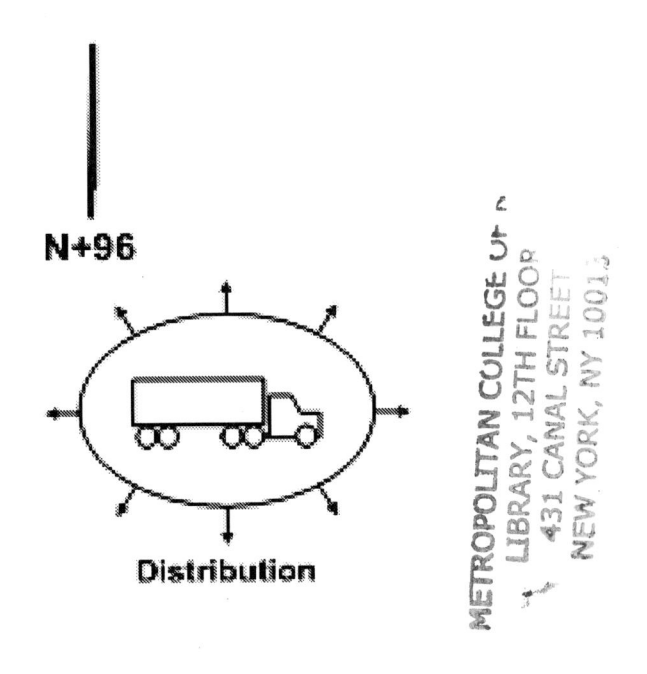

N+96

Distribution

CHAPTER 10

Sustainment of Disaster Operations

Stage III: Sustainment of Disaster Operations

The Sustainment of Disaster Operations (N+120 – N+ End State hours) is the first time in the whole process we see the disaster environment begin to stabilize which will provide the staff and relief personnel to develop a staff rhythm. This continuity allows the workforce to predict and eventually get ahead of the relief support required, ultimately moving the supported communities that much closer to recovery.

The establishment of in-transit visibility gives the staffs the ability to manage supply flow and initiate the redistribution of commodities across supported regions and distribution points. The coordinated redistribution between Distribution Points of other areas or regions is the beginning of the operations to achieve closure. As we have already discussed, most operations will consist of a series of linear distribution networks, which act independently to one another mainly do to debris blocking the roadways and no consistent reporting flow identifying required commodities need and excess quantities available. Once this lateral redistribution of supplies begins, the operation has moved to the next level in maturity demonstrating that the state and local authorities can start to take more control of their own communities, moving one step closer to end state.

Somewhere early in the Sustainment Operation the different staff authorities should initiate the development of a Closure Plan that can be agreed on between the different levels of government and civilian

James H. Henderson

agencies, and that can be executable at all levels and can continue after the Sustainment and Closure Stages are complete. The complete Stage III: Sustainment of Disaster Operations (N+120 – N+ End State hours) visible in its entirety below in Figure 35.

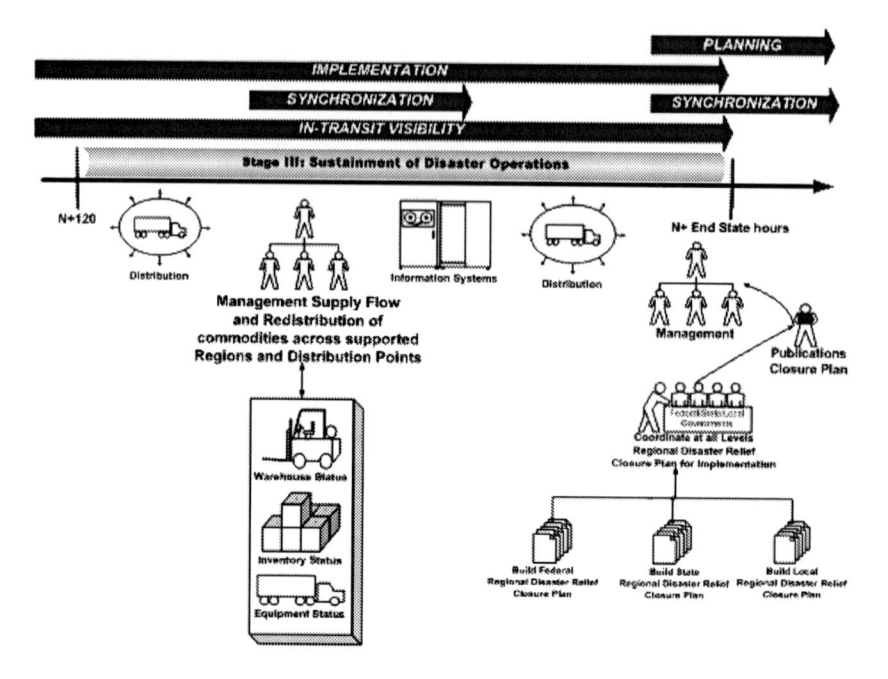

Figure 35, Stage III: Sustainment of Disaster Operations

Synchronization and Implementation

The key of this phase is the beginning of the redistribution process, which moves us closer to end state. The following Stage III – Synchronization and Implementation Objective Checklist and Diagram Insert (See Figure 36) provided for review:

- <u>Stage III– Synchronization and Implementation</u>

Objective Checklist

1. Management of Supply Flow.

2. Conduct Redistribution of commodities across supported Regions and Distribution Points
3. Manage Warehouse, Inventory, and Equipment Status.
4. Conduct Redistribution, as necessary, of support supplies, equipment, and personnel.
5. Coordinate, as necessary, the redistribution of contracted resources.

Stage III– Synchronization and Implementation Diagram Insert, Figure 36

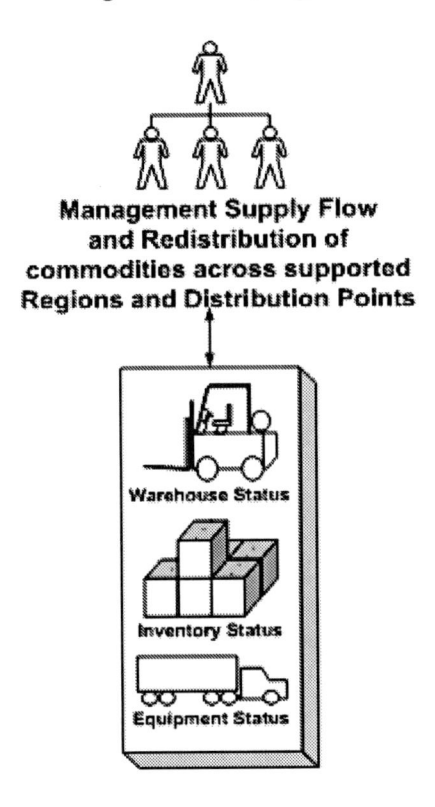

Management Supply Flow and Redistribution of commodities across supported Regions and Distribution Points

Warehouse Status

Inventory Status

Equipment Status

In-Transit Visibility

Utilizing automated Command and Control Information Systems staffs must have situational awareness of the Disaster Relief Distribution Network to; (1) anticipate logistical needs (2) integrate supply and services (3) synchronize logistical support to facilitate priorities and (4) optimize assets for present and future operational support.

Remember the importance of In-Transit Visibility to provide staff sections visibility of movement, the capacity of supply nodes, and the control over the network. This has been covered in both Stages I and II and must continue throughout the process. The following Stage III – In-Transit Visibility Objective Checklist and Diagram Insert (See Figure 37) provided for review:

- *Stage III– In-Transit Visibility Objective Checklist*

<u>This is the same checklist from Stages I and II and is still as essential here in Stage III</u>

1. Provide Command and Control of the Disaster Relief Distribution Network, by the Management of Information Systems to give visibility of assets and commodities as they move across the network.
2. Conduct distribution tracking of convoys and commodities as it moves across the Disaster Relief Distribution Network. Example of types of hardware that could be utilized consist of the following:
   a. Convoys
   - Satellite Communications – Capability to receive data from mobile transponders and send to information system for tracking.
   - Transponders
     - MTS – Movement Tracking System
     - DTRACS – Defense Tracking System
     - DynaFleet – Volvo Commercial System
     - PanaTracker – Commercial System
     - VISTAR – Commercial System
     - Cell Phone Tracking Capability
   b. Commodities
   - Satellite Communications – Capability to receive data from fixed or hand-held interrogators and send to information system for tracking.
   - RFID - Radio Frequency Identification Devices

Logistics in Support of Disaster Relief

- Transponders Tags (Sustainment and Vehicle)
- Antennas
- Radio Frequency Modules
- Readers
- Software
- Bar Code Labels
- Fixed Interrogator
- Hand-held Interrogators
- Early Entry Deployment Support Kit (EEDSK)

Stage III– In-Transit Visibility Diagram Insert, Figure 37

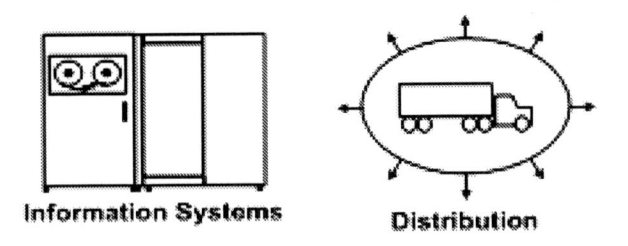

Information Systems   Distribution

Planning

Staff coordination and hard work is required to develop a Disaster Relief Closure Plan in a short time frame for implementation and successful execution. The following Stage III – Planning and Synchronization 1 Objective Checklist and Diagram Insert (See Figure 38) provided for review:

- *Stage III– Planning Objective Checklist*
    1. Develop a comprehensive Regional Disaster Relief Closure Plan, incorporating feedback and identifying tasks and responsibility at all levels (Federal/State/Local Government).
    2. Coordinate at all Levels Regional Disaster Relief Closure Plan for Implementation.

3. Produce and distribute publications of the approved Disaster Relief Closure Plan to all levels of government and civilian agencies.
4. Management the implementation until the operation is complete.

Stage III– Planning Diagram Insert, Figure 38

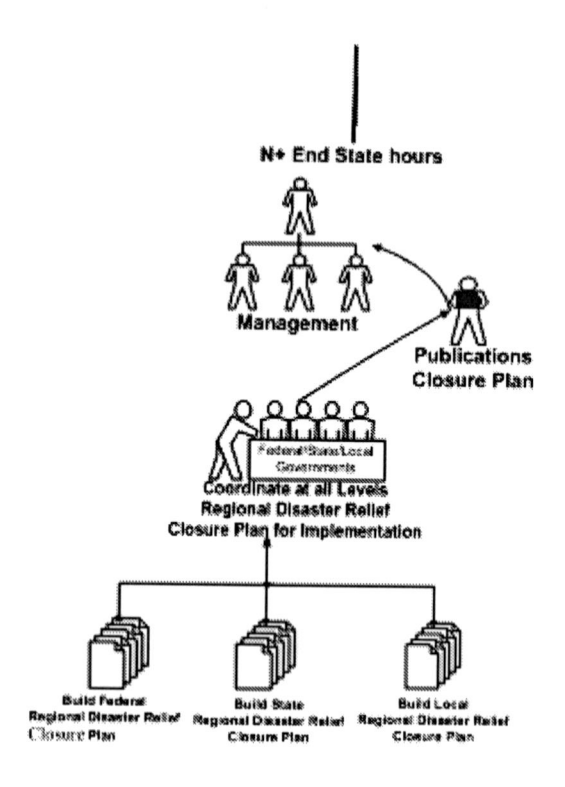

CHAPTER 11

Closure of Disaster Operations

Stage IV: Closure of Disaster Operations

The Closure of Disaster Operations (N+ End State hours – N+ Closure-one week after completion) is the last stage to be conducted, and centers on the Management of Supply Flow and the Retrograde of commodities and personnel forward across supported Regions and Distribution Points.

Once the situation is at a stable point in the operation, the Closure Plan should be initiated, and activation of stand-down notification will start.

Upon completion of relief support operations the government and civilian agencies at all levels come together to conduct an After Action Review (AAR), results and lesson learned are published, and the Disaster Relief Support Plans are updated at all levels. The complete Stage IV: Closure of Disaster Operations

(N+ End State hours – N+ Closure-one week after completion) is visible in its entirety below in Figure 39.

James H. Henderson

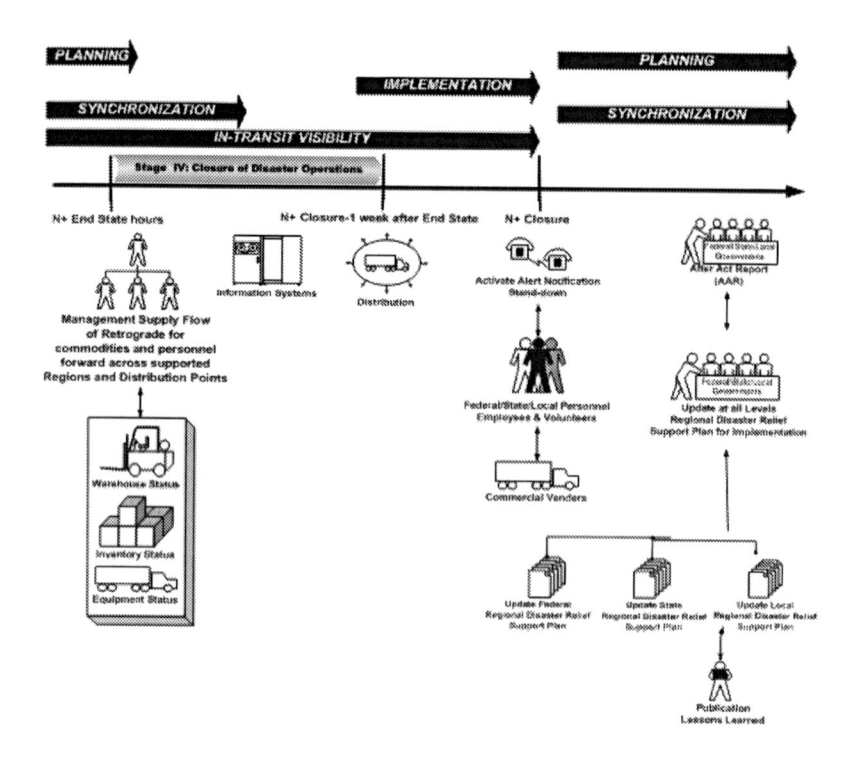

Figure 39, Stage IV: Closure of Disaster Operations

Planning and Synchronization 1

The Management of Supply Flow and the Retrograde of commodities and personnel consist of not only relief commodities, but also support resources consisting of people and equipment, as well as facilities utilized to support the sustainment infrastructure. There could be requirements for the commodities to be sent to a staging location for packing and onward movement in support of the same or different disaster locations. This not just restricted to commodities, but could encompass people and equipment, which very well could be of limited supply or availability. The following Stage IV – Planning and Synchronization 1 Objective Checklist and Diagram Insert (See Figure 40) provided for review:

- *Stage IV – Planning and Synchronization 1*
  <u>Objective Checklist</u>

Logistics in Support of Disaster Relief

1. Management Supply Flow.
2. Conduct Retrograde of commodities across supported Regions and Distribution Points
3. Manage Warehouse, Inventory, and Equipment Status.
4. Conduct Retrograde, as depicted of support supplies, equipment, and personnel.
5. Close facilities and contracted resources in accordance with Closure Plan.

Stage IV – Planning and Synchronization 1 Diagram Insert, Figure 40

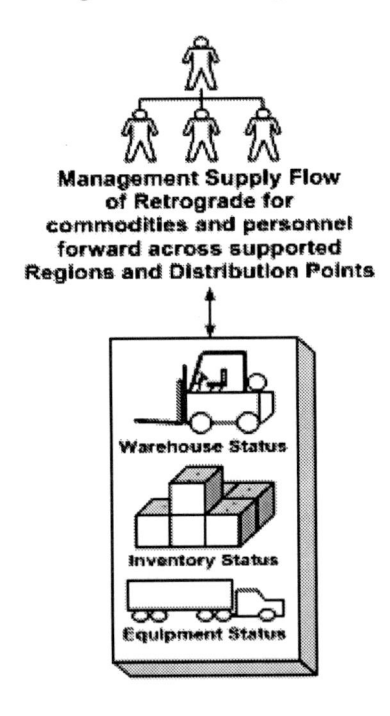

In-Transit Visibility

Utilizing automated Command and Control Information Systems staffs can have situational awareness of the Disaster Relief Distribution Network to; (1) anticipate logistical needs (2) integrate supply and services (3) synchronize logistical support to facilitate priorities and (4) optimize assets for present and future operational support. In-Transit Visibility provides staff sections visibility of movement, the capacity of supply nodes, and the control over the network. The information is still the same, in that the basic technology is the Transponders or Interrogators send data which channels down finally to feed the command and control information systems. The following Stage IV – In-Transit Visibility Objective Checklist and Diagram Insert (See Figure 41) provided for review:

- *Stage IV – In-Transit Visibility Objective Checklist*
1. Provide Command and Control of the Disaster Relief Distribution Network, by the Management of Information Systems to give visibility of assets and commodities as they move across the network. The basic technology is the same for all the stages and it outlined in detail earlier in this book,
2. Conduct distribution tracking of convoys and commodities as it moves across the Disaster Relief Distribution Network. Example of types of hardware that could be utilized consist of the following:
   a. Convoys
     - Satellite Communications – Capability to receive data from mobile transponders and send to information system for tracking.
     - Transponders
       - MTS – Movement Tracking System
       - DTRACS – Defense Tracking System
       - DynaFleet – Volvo Commercial System
       - PanaTracker – Commercial System
       - VISTAR – Commercial System
       - Cell Phone Tracking Capability
   b. Commodities
     - Satellite Communications – Capability to receive data from fixed or hand-held interrogators and send to information system for tracking.
     - RFID - Radio Frequency Identification Devices
       - Transponders Tags (Sustainment and Vehicle)
       - Antennas
       - Radio Frequency Modules
       - Readers

Logistics in Support of Disaster Relief

- Software
- Bar Code Labels
- Fixed Interrogator
- Hand-held Interrogators
- Early Entry Deployment Support Kit (EEDSK)

Stage IV – In-Transit Visibility Diagram Insert Figure 41

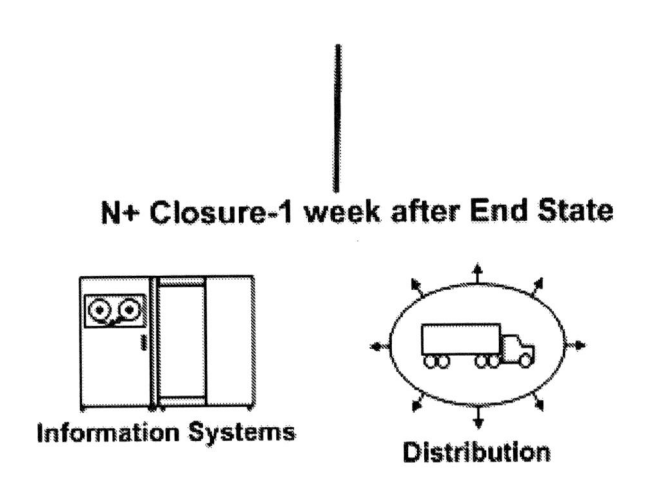

N+ Closure-1 week after End State

Information Systems   **Distribution**

Implementation

Once the situation is at a stable point in the operation, the Closure Plan initiates, and activation of stand-down notification starts. This requires a timeline established between federal, state, and local employees, as well as volunteers, private organizations, and commercial venders that depicts "Who" and "When" certain operations and organizations conclude relief support. Examples of these agencies and organization:

- *Federal* - U.S. Army, Air Force, Navy, Marine, and Coast Guard Active Forces units, Federal Emergency Management Agency (FEMA), and Federal Law enforcement Agencies.
- *State* - National Guard units (Army and Air Force), State Emergency Management and State Law enforcement Agencies, and other agencies under their control assigned a task or duty within the Disaster Relief Support Plan.
- *Local* – Government and County employees and facilities, Law enforcement and Fire Departments, and other agencies

under their control assigned a task or duty within the Disaster Relief Support Plan.
- *Volunteers and Private Organizations* - Local Hospitals, Church Groups, Non-profit Groups, Companies, etc., and the Red Cross to name a few.
- *Commercial Venders* – Business, Trucking Companies, contracted or not, providing support for the relief effort.

The following Stage IV – Implementation Objective Checklist and Diagram Insert provided for review:

- *Stage IV – Implementation Objective Checklist*
1. Activate Alert Notification Stand-down.
2. Notification includes all Federal/State/Local Personnel Employees & Volunteers as depicted in timeline.
3. Notify all Commercial Venders in support of relief operations on timeline for conclusion of contract.

Stage IV – Implementation Diagram Insert, Figure 42

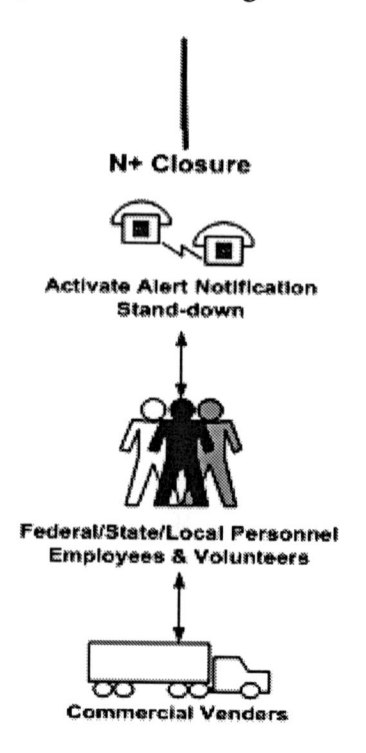

N+ Closure

Activate Alert Notification Stand-down

Federal/State/Local Personnel Employees & Volunteers

Commercial Venders

Planning and Synchronization 2

After completion of relief operations the government and civilian agencies at all levels come together to conduct an After Action Review (AAR). From the results of this review a lessons learned document is published reflecting on all aspects of the operations and providing beneficial feedback of not just problems and concerns, but also should include the good things that occurred, as well as things that should have occurred. After all feedback verified and evaluated the Disaster Relief Support Plans are update at all levels. The following Stage IV – Planning and Synchronization Objective Checklist and Diagram Insert (See Figure 43) provided for review:

- *Stage IV – Planning and Synchronization 2*

Objective Checklist

1. Conduct an After Action Review (AAR) evolving all levels (federal, state, local, and Volunteers and Private Organizations.
2. Publish a lessons learned document reflecting on all aspects of the operations.
3. Update the Disaster Relief Support Plan, at all Levels.
4. Produce and distribute publications of the approved Disaster Relief Updated Support Plan to all levels of government and civilian agencies.

James H. Henderson

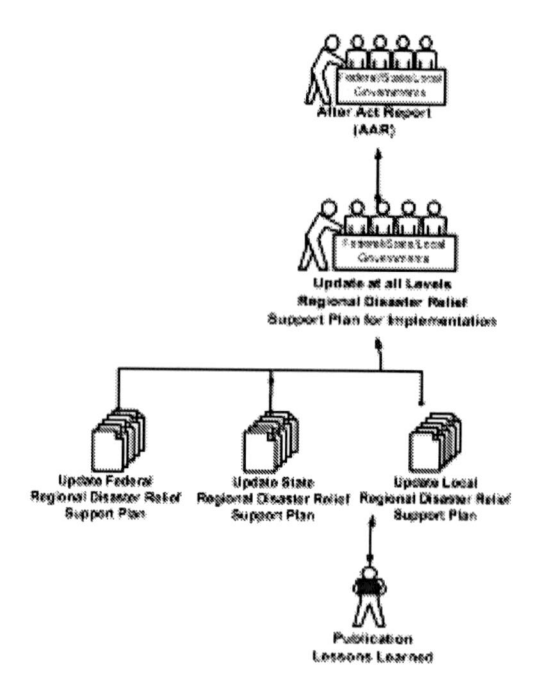

Stage IV – Planning and Synchronization 2 Diagram Insert, Figure 43

CHAPTER 12

Thinking Out of the Box

Perception

There is an old saying, "You have to spend money to make money", and the biggest question in anticipation of disaster relief support is how much time and money are you able to spend in precautionary work. The money spent for planning, coordination, and preparatory support in anticipation of a disaster must be cost effective and worth the investment. It can be thought of as if buying a term life insurance policy when you spend the money up front hoping you never have to claim the benefits. The key is to spend as little as possible before the disaster and at the same time to make sure the money that is spent is the most productive. This money spent will be in the form of people's time and salaries, as well as purchasing of equipment and services to be utilized prior and during disaster relief operations.

As stated previously, planning, coordination, and training play the largest role in having a successful outcome.

There are many organizations or agencies that could and should review their policies and procedures as well as what could be done prior to a disaster in evacuating the contents of key facilities and office buildings. Examples of these types of facilities are libraries, museums, and government facilities that need a plan in place to move and or safeguard their contents prior to the disaster. This could be money well spent and should be considered.

Libraries, Museums, and Government Facilities

When we talk about libraries, museums, and Government Facilities, we are really talking about those things that are valuable or irreplaceable, the kind of items a person would purchase insurance on in the anticipation of a disaster. Using the analogy above libraries and museums would fit into an example of facilities that might purchase services and equipment in support of the evacuation of artifacts and literature. The question is to what extent and magnitude do you lean forward in the saddle. One key is how important it is and how much prior notice do you have to execute such a plan. How much prior notice you will have can never be answered, but the importance of it must be gauged. With all that said, let us review a library or museum for ways to enhance a smooth evacuation. From reading Chapter 6, Building the Relief Support Network, you should remember the importance of bar code labels, RIFD tags, interrogators, transponders, and command and control software systems. This type of equipment and technology utilizing anyone of the items, a combination, or all could assist in the smooth evacuation and change of custody of artifacts for shipment, tracking, and identification. Most libraries and museums have some sort of bar code labeling system, which assists in their existing inventories, as well as issuing and receiving of items. A system like this that is already in place can be the platform to build shipping manifests for crating and boxing of items for evacuation. These automated manifests are then burned to the RIFD tags and devices attached to shipment. If you do not already have an automated system to develop the manifest then the information can be manually imputed to the tag. The next step is to plan for the proper number of containers required to move the items. This could require some specially made crates to transport the artifacts safely. All these details can be contracted in advance, and the proper coordination made so when you activate the contract they already know the requirement, are aware of the short timeframe, and the urgency of the mission. The final thing to consider is where you would want the items stored. At this point, a workable plan is in order. Simply implement and track.

Simulation Training

In Chapter 3, The Plan, we discussed that planning is only as good as its execution, and to make a plan successful there requires a need for coordination and training so all players know and can work toward the prescribed outcome. In the Chapter 3, I give an example of a Band of Support relating to coordination at different levels to achieve a support network that ultimately could assist the entire state with some level of support. The importance of coordination and training is evident in any operation. Coordination is self-explanatory and I think all of us understand the need, but training entails individual, as well as collective training involving other organizations and agencies. Individual training is easier for an organization to administer and is an initial requirement before any collective training could be conducted effectively. The collective training that we are discussing is more complex in that it involves more than one organization and agencies, and a shorter timeframe to execute.

The Army has been successful over the last ten years in utilizing modeling and simulation technology to facilitate training between two or more different units to enhance training of upcoming operations. This training utilizes computer-generated scenarios, which support the training audience mission and involves real people making decisions from the data provide by the simulation and/or their injection of input into the scenario for the simulation to carry out. These types of simulation training exercises can be developed to support individual or collective training requirements. There are many companies today developing stand-alone computer training software, which can put the trainee in a certain situations or scenarios, and have them work through a series of tasks reinforcing training techniques and procedures. There is also a simulation exercise geared toward a collective training base, which supports multi-echelon training where a scenario can be developed that involves federal, state, local, and volunteer organizations training for potential disaster relief operations. Training of this kind would assist greatly in the development of new ideas and ways to better support relief operations.

Summary

The above chapters have outlined some new ideas and concepts for implementation, or more importantly just to stimulate the brain. I believe the main point to arrive from this work is that a plan is required to successfully implement support operations during a disaster. Moreover, a plan is only as good as its execution. Plans can look good on paper, but may not be executable. Planning, coordination, and training are required for a successful operation. Prior planning and anticipation are needed for an operation of this magnitude to be successful. It is my sincere hope that others will use this information and improve upon it for my reason for this work is that we must start in order to finish. Remember, if this were easy then they would not call it a disaster.

BIBLIOGRAPHY

The bibliography lists field manuals by new number followed by old number.

Joint publications

CJCSI 3121.01A. *Standing Rules of Engagement for US Forces* (U). 01 Sep.1999.

CJCSM 3113.01. *Th eater Engagement Planning.* 01 Feb. 1998.

CJCSM 3500.04B. *Universal Joint Task List.* 01 Oct. 1999.

Joint Doctrine Encyclopedia. 16 Jul. 1997.

Joint Military Operations Historical Collection. 15 Jul. 1997.

JP 0-2. *Unified Action Armed Forces* (UNAAF). 24 Feb. 1995.

JP 1-0. *Doctrine for Personnel Support to Joint Operations.* 19 Nov. 1998.

JP 1-02. *Department of Defense Dictionary of Military and Associated Terms.* Available online at http://www.dtic.mil/doctrine/jel/doddict/

JP 1-05. *Religious Ministry Support for Joint Operations.* 26 Aug. 1996.

JP 1-06. *Joint Tactics, Techniques, and Procedures for Financial Management During Joint Operations.* 22 Dec. 1999.

JP 2-0. *Doctrine for Intelligence Support to Joint Operations.* 09 Mar. 2000.

JP 3-0. *Doctrine for Joint Operations.* 1 Feb. 1995.

JP 3-07. *Joint Doctrine for Military Operations Other Th an War.* 16 Jun. 1995.

JP 3-07.1. *Joint Tactics, Techniques, and Procedures for Foreign Internal Defense* (FID). 26 Jun. 1996.

JP 3-07.2. *Joint Tactics, Techniques, and Procedures for Antiterrorism.* 17 Mar. 1998.

JP 3-07.3. *Joint Tactics, Techniques, and Procedures for Peace Operations.* 12 Feb. 1999.

JP 3-07.4. *Joint Counter drug Operations.* 17 Feb. 1998.

JP 3-07.5. *Joint Tactics, Techniques, and Procedures for Noncombatant Evacuation Operations.* 30 Sep. 1997.

JP 3-07.7. *Joint Tactics, Techniques, and Procedures for Domestic Support Operations.* TBP.

JP 3-08. *Interagency Coordination During Joint Operations.* 2 volumes. 9 Oct. 1996.

JP 3-09. *Doctrine for Joint Fire Support.* 12 May 1998.

JP 3-11. *Joint Doctrine for Operations in Nuclear, Biological, and Chemical (NBC) Environments.* 11 Jul. 2000.

JP 3-13. *Joint Doctrine for Information Operations.* 9 Oct. 1998.

JP 3-14. *Joint Doctrine for Space Operations.* TBP.

JP 3-16. *Joint Doctrine for Multinational Operations.* 05 Apr. 2000.

JP 3-18. *Joint Doctrine for Forcible Entry Operations.* TBP.

JP 3-33. *Joint Force Capabilities.* 13 Oct. 1999.

JP 3-35. *Joint Deployment and Redeployment Operations.* 7 Sep. 1999.

JP 3-53. *Doctrine for Joint Psychological Operations.* 10 Jul. 1996.

JP 3-54. *Joint Doctrine for Operations Security.* 24 Jan. 1997.

JP 3-55. *Doctrine for Reconnaissance, Surveillance, and Target Acquisition Support for Joint Operations.* 14 Apr. 1993.

JP 3-57. *Doctrine for Joint Civil Affairs.* 21 Jun. 1995.

JP 3-58. *Joint Doctrine for Military Deception.* 31 May 1996.

JP 3-59. *Joint Doctrine, Tactics, Techniques, and Procedure for Meteorological and Oceanographic Support.* 23 Mar. 1999.

JP 3-60. *Joint Doctrine for Targeting.* TBP.

JP 3-61. *Doctrine for Public Affairs in Joint Operations.* 14 May 1997.

JP 4-0. *Doctrine for Logistic Support of Joint Operations.* 06 Apr. 2000.

JP 4-01. *Joint Doctrine for the Defense Transportation System.* 17 Jun. 1997.

JP 4-01.6. *Joint Tactics, Techniques, and Procedures for Joint Logistics Over the Shore.* 12 Nov. 1998

JP 4-01.8. *Joint Tactics, Techniques, and Procedures for Joint Reception, Staging, Onward Movement, and Integration.* 13 Jun. 2000.

JP 4-02. *Doctrine for Health Service Support in Joint Operations.* 26 Apr. 1995.

JP 4-03. *Joint Bulk Petroleum Doctrine.* 25 Jul. 1995.

JP 4-04. *Joint Doctrine for Civil Engineering Support.* 26 Sep. 1995.

JP 4-05. *Joint Doctrine for Mobilization Planning.* 22 Jun. 1995.

JP 4-06. *JTTP for Mortuary Affairs in Joint Operations.* 28 Aug. 1996.

JP 4-07. *Joint Tactics, Techniques, and Procedures for Common User Logistics During Joint Operations.* TPB.

JP 4-08. *Joint Doctrine for Logistic Support of Multinational Operations.* TBP.

JP 5-0. *Doctrine for Planning Joint Operations.* 13 Apr. 1995.

JP 5-03.1. *Joint Operation Planning and Execution System, Volume I (Planning and Procedures)*. 04 Aug. 1993.

ARMY PUBLICATIONS

AR 71-9. Materiel Requirements. 30 Apr. 1997. Available online at http://books.usapa.belvoir.army.mil/cgi-bin/ bookmgr/ BOOKS/ R71_9/CCONTENTS

DA Memo 10-1. *Executive Agent Responsibilities assigned to the Secretary of the Army*. 15 Jan. 1997.

FM 1 (FM 100-1). *Th e Army*. 14 Jun. 1994.

FM 1-0 (FM 12-6). *Personnel Doctrine*. 09 Sep. 94.

FM 1-04 (FM 27-100). *Legal Support to Operations*. 01 Mar. 2000.

FM 1-05 (FM 16-1). *Religious Support*. 26 May 1995.

FM 1-06 (FM 14-100). *Financial Management Operations*. 07 May 1997.

FM 1-08 (FM 12-50). *U.S. Army Bands*. 15 Oct. 1999.

FM 2-0 (FM 34-1). *Intelligence and Electronic Warfare Operations*. 27 Sep. 1994.

FM 2-01.3 (FM 34-130). *Intelligence Preparation of the Battlefi eld*. 08 Jul. 1994.

FM 2-33.2 (FM 34-81). *Weather Support for Army Tactical Operations*. 31 Aug. 1989.

FM 3-0 (formally FM 100-5), *Operations*. 14 June 2001, 12-6.

FM 3-01.94 (FM 44-94). *Army Air and Missile Defense Command Operations*. 31 Mar. 2000.

FM 3-04.500 (FM 1-500). *Army Aviation Maintenance*. 27 Jan. 1995.

FM 3-05 (FM 100-25). *Doctrine for Army Special Operations Forces*. 01 Aug. 1999.

FM 3-05.30 (FM 33-1). *Psychological Operations*. 01 Jun. 2000.

FM 3-06 (FM 90-10). *Military Operations on Urbanized Terrain (MOUT) (How to Fight).* 15 Aug. 1979.

FM 3-07 (FM 100-20). *Military Operations in Low Intensity Conflict.* 05 Dec. 1990. When revised, FM 3-07 will be renamed Stability Operations and Support Operations.

FM 3-07.2. *Force Protection.* TBP.

FM 3-07.3 (FM 100-23). *Peace Operations.* 30 Dec. 1994.

FM 3-07.6 (FM 100-23). *HA_ Multi-service Procedures for Humanitarian Assistance Operations.* 31 Oct. 1994.

FM 3-07.7 (FM 100-19). *Domestic Support Operations.* 01 Jul. 1993.

FM 3-09 (FM 6-20). *Fire Support in the Air Land Battle.* 17 May 1988.

FM 3-11 (FM 3-100). *Chemical Operations Principles and Fundamentals.* 08 May 1996.

FM 3-11.4 (FM 3-4). *NBC Protection.* 29 May 1992.

FM 3-11.14 (FM 3-14). *Nuclear, Biological, and Chemical(NBC) Vulnerability Analysis.* 12 Nov. 1997.

FM 3-13 (FM 100-6). *Information Operations.* 27 Aug. 1996.

FM 3-14 (FM 100-18). *Space Support to Army Operations.* 20 Jul. 1995.

FM 3-16 (FM 100-8). *The Army in Multinational Operations.* 24 Nov. 1997.

FM 3-34.250 (FM 5-104). *General Engineering.* 12 Nov. 1986.

FM 3-35 (FM 100-17). *Mobilization, Deployment, Redeployment, Demobilization.* 28 Oct. 1992.

FM 3-35.1 (FM 100-17-1). *Army Pre-Positioned Afloat Operations.* 27 Jul. 1996.

FM 3-35.2 (FM 100-17-2). *Army Pre-Positioned Land.* 16 Feb. 1999.

FM 3-35.5 (FM 100-17-5). *Redeployment.* 29 Sep. 1999.

FM 3-55. *Reconnaissance Operations.* TBP.

FM 3-57 (FM 41-10). *Civil Affairs Operations.* 11 Jan. 1993.

FM 3-60 (FM 6-20-10). *Tactics, Techniques, and Procedures for the Targeting Process.* 08 May 1996.

FM 3-90. *Tactics.* TBP.

FM 3-100.7 (FM 100-7). *Decisive Force: The Army in Theater Operations.* 31 May 1995.

FM 3-100.11 (FM 100-11). *Force Integration.* 15 Jan. 1998.

FM 3-100.14 (FM 100-14). *Risk Management.* 23 Apr. 1998.

FM 3-100.16 (FM 100-16). *Army Operational Support.* 31 May 1995. FM 3-100.16 will be superseded by portions of

FM 3-100.7 and FM 4-0 when these manuals are republished.

FM 3-100.21 (FM 100-21). *Contractors on the Battlefield.* 26 Mar. 2000.

FM 3-100.22 (FM 100-22). *Installation Management.* 11 Oct.1994.

FM 3-100.38 (FM 100-38). *UXO Multi-service Procedures for Operations in an Unexploded Ordnance Environment.* 10 Jul. 1996.

FM 4-0 (FM 100-10). *Combat Service Support.* 03 Oct. 1995.

FM 4-01 (FM 55-1). *Transportation Operations.* 03 Oct. 1995.

FM 4-01.4 (FM 100-10-1). *Th eater Distribution.* 01 Oct. 1999.

FM 4-01.8 (FM 100-17-3). *Reception, Staging, Onward*

FM 4-02 (FM 8-10). *Health Service Support in a Theater of Operations.* 01 Mar. 1991.

FM 4-20 (FM 10-1). *Quartermaster Principles.* 11 Aug. 1994.

FM 4-30.2 (FM 9-43-1). *Maintenance Operations and Procedures.* 21 Feb. 1997.

FM 4-30.11 (FM 21-16). *Unexploded Ordnance (UXO) Procedures.* 30 Aug. 1994.

FM 4-30.12 (FM 9-15). *Explosive Ordnance Disposal Service and Unit Operations.* 08 May 1996.

FM 4-93.4 (FM 63-4). *Combat Service Support Operations–Theater Army Area Command.* 24 Sep. 1984.

FM 4-100.2 (FM 100-10-2). *Contracting Support on the Battlefield.* 04 Aug. 1999.

FM 4-100.9 (FM 100-9). *Reconstitution.* 13 Jan. 1992.

FM 5-0 (FM 101-5). *Staff Organizations and Operations.* 31 May 1997. When revised, FM 5-0 will be renamed Planning.

FM 6-0. *Command and Control.* TBP.

FM 6-22 (FM 22-100). *Army Leadership.* 31 Aug. 1999.

FM 7-0 (FM 25-100). *Training the Force.* 15 Nov. 1988.

FM 7-10 (FM 25-101). *Battle Focused Training.* 30 Sep. 1990.

FM 7-15. *Army Universal Task List (AUTL).* TBP.

DEPARTMENT OF DEFENSE PUBLICATIONS

DOD Directives available online at http://web7.whs.osd.mil/corres.htm

DOD *Civil Disturbance Plan, Annex C (Concept of Operations), Appendix 8 (Special Instructions),* 15 Feb. 1991; modified by Director of Military Support message 161639Z Jul. 96, Subject: Changes to DOD Civil Disturbance

DODD 3025.15. *Military Assistance to Civil Authorities.* 18 Feb. 1997.

DODD 3100.10. *Space Policy.* 09 Jul. 1999.

DODD 5100.1. *Functions of the Department of Defense and Its Major Components.* 25 Sep. 1987.

DODD 5100.46. *Foreign Disaster Relief.* 4 Dec. 1975.

DODD 5160.54. *Critical Asset Assurance Program (CAAP)*. 20 Jan. 1998.

DODD 5525.5. *DOD Cooperation with Civilian Law Enforcement Officials*. 15 Jan. 1986.

"*DOD Principles of Information.*" Washington, D.C.:

Government Printing Office, 01 Apr. 1997. Available online at http://www/defenselink.mil/admin/about.html#PrinInfo

National Military Strategy of the United States of America, 1997. Available online at http://www.dtic.mil/jcs/nms

PUBLIC LAWS AND OTHER PUBLICATIONS

The United States Code is available online at http://uscode.house.gov/usc.htm

Arms Export Control Act (Public Law 90-629, Oct. 22, 1968, [82 Stat. 1320]; see Title 22 USC, section 2751, Short Title note).

Authority to Use Army and Air National Guard in Certain

Counter-drug Operations (Title 32 USC, section 112).

Civil Military Cooperation Action Program (Title 10 USC, section 401).

Defense Against Weapons of Mass Destruction Act of 1996 (Public Law 104-201, section xiv [110 Stat. 2422]). Available online at http://www.access.gpo.gov/nara/publaw/104publ.html

Federal-Aid Highway Act of 1956, Creating the Interstate System: Public Roads, v. 60, no. 1, http://www.tfhrc.gov/pubrds/summer96/p96su10.htm

Federal Response Plan. Available online at http://www.fema.gov/r-n-r/frp

Foreign Assistance Act of 1961 (Public. Law 87-195, Sept. 4, 1961, [75 Stat. 424]; see Title 22 USC, section 2151, Short Title note).

Goldwater-Nichols Department of Defense Reorganization Act of 1986 (Title 10 USC, Subtitle A, Part I, Chapter 5). Available online at http://dtic.mil/jcs/core/title_10.html

Joint Vision 2010 (Washington, DC: Joint Chiefs of Staff, 1995), 24. Insurrection Act (Title 10 USC, Chapter 15).

Military Support for Civilian Law Enforcement Agencies (Title 10 USC, sections 371-382, Chapter 18).

National Security Act of 1947 (61 Stat. 495, chapter 343; see Title 50 USC, section 401, Short Title note).

National Security Decision Directive 221, Narcotics and National Security, 08 Apr. 1986.

Posse Comitatus Act (Title 18 USC, section 1385).

Robert T. Stafford Disaster Relief and Emergency Assistance Act (Title 42 USC, sections 5142–5203).

Title 10 USC, Annex B, section 3013 (responsibilities of the secretary of the Army).

U.S. Department of Transportation, Federal Highway Administration, http://www.fhwa.dot.gov/hep10/nhs/

Wikipedia, the free encyclopedia, *Interstate Highway System*, http://en.wikipedia.org/wiki/Interstate_highway

GLOSSARY

Abbreviations and Acronyms

AO	Area of Operation
BCS3	Battle Command Sustainment Support System
CFA	Call Forward Area
COA	Course of Action
FARE	Forward Area Refueling Equipment
FAWPSS	Forward Area Water Point Supply System
FDP	Forward Distribution Point
FEMA	Federal Emergency Management Agency
FL	Forklift
FSSP	Fuel System Supply Point
FST	Forward Surgical Team
HMMWV	High-Mobility Multipurpose-Wheeled Vehicle
HRT	Highway Regulating Team
ISB	Intermediate Staging Base
ITV	In-Transit Visibility
MCB	Movement Control Battalion
MCT	Movement Control Team
MDMP	Military Decision Making Process
MILVAN	Military-Owned Demountable Container
NCO	Non-Commissioned Officer
NGO	Non-Governmental Organization
PAX	Passengers

PLS	Palletized Loading System
POL	Petroleum, Oils, and Lubricants
RFID	Radio Frequency Identification Devices
ROWPU	Reverse Osmosis Water Purification Unit
RT	Rough-Terrain
RTFL	Rough-Terrain Forklift
SC (E)	Sustainment Command (Expeditionary)
SMFT	Semi Trailer-Mounted Fabric Tank
SOP	Standard Operating Procedure
TEMPER	Tent, Expandable, Modular, Personnel
TTP	Training, Techniques, and Procedures

About The Author

Lieutenant Colonel Henderson was commissioned a 2d Lieutenant and assigned to the Quartermaster following completion of his Master Degree from University of Southern Mississippi in May 1985. He is also a graduate of the United States Army Command and General Staff College, the Quartermaster Officer Basic Course and Quartermaster Officer Advanced Course.

Lieutenant Colonel James H. Henderson has severed tours in Operations Desert Shield and Storm, as well as Operations Iraqi Freedom II (OIF II). He retired from active duty on 1 August 2005, and is now working as a consultant for the Army's logistical automation systems the Battle Command Sustainment Support System (BCS3) and the Transportation Coordinators-Automated Information for Movements System II (TC-AIMS II). Mr. Henderson is the author of the book, "*The Process of Military Distribution Management; A Guide to Assist Military and Civilian Logisticians in Linking Commodities and Movement.*" He conducts classes and seminars for the U.S. Army Quartermaster and Transportation Schools, as well as instructs National Guard and Reserve units on Distribution Management and Logistical Support to Disaster Relief at Camp Shelby, Mississippi. He deployed to the State of Louisiana for Hurricane Katrina in support of 13 SC(E), located at Fort Hood, Texas as a contractor and representative of BCS3. That is where he gained the knowledge and experience to develop the ideas and procedures for logistical support to disaster relief operations.

CPSIA information can be obtained at www.ICGtesting.com
Printed in the USA
BVOW04*0736021115

425187BV00005B/14/P